Read My Song,
Read My Heart,
Read My Soul

The Secret Messages in Your Favorite Song

Awen Finn

Studio 8 Publishing

SYDNEY

For my three personal angels,
Michael, Thomas and Reilly

All My Love

"I am the Cosmic Ocean of sound and the little wave of the body
vibration in it."
-PARAMAHANSA YOGANANDA

"Color is the keyboard, the eyes are the hammers, and the soul is the
piano with many strings.
The artist is the hand which plays, touching one key or another, to
cause vibrations in the soul."
-WASSILY KANDINSKY

Praise for

Read My Song, Read My Heart, Read My Soul

Here are what some of my clients have to say about their Song Read:

"It was so beautiful, very, very good and spot on…and made me wonder at the subtleties and hidden messages in this song which I hadn't thought about very much and not at all on this level. You're on to an incredible tool for offering insights on a completely new level."

"Thank you so much for this. I just love the explanation. It rings very true for me. Much love, xx."

"I love this! You did such a great job. Thank you :) I have already recommended you to my aunt and a friend, just seconds after reading it. That is just, amazing. I love it."

"Wow! Your analysis was really fantastic and accurate. The way you analyze music is very interesting and admirable for me, a writer, a musician and a person. What you've written not only applies to me but also the song. I'm seeing this band in July and this analysis will make their performance even more special."

"Well you were pretty much dead on. I thought that was a pretty good reading altogether…and I have had a lot of readings in my time. I'm quite "psychic" myself. I'm pretty surprised you can get all that from a song. Good going. Thank you for it and all the best!"

"Thank you for your reply, you are accurate in what your music reading has uncovered, I never thought so many things could be uncovered by a song, although I adore my music and different songs generate different emotions and levels of happiness or sadness for me, so it makes sense that we connect with lyrics and instrumental music."

"First let me thank you for taking the time to analyze my choice of song, I found it to be clear, precise and frankly quite accurate. I especially liked and respect your spiritual approach. May I ask you about your obvious gifts you have in the field? I found your take to be very accurate, rather penetrating and sympathetic. How could I not agree with your kind comments!"

"Wow very interesting stuff. Most of what you said I was able to relate to very well. I'm sure there is plenty of truth in this reading, amazingly accurate in the earlier part of the reading. Happy to have taken part, it was very interesting. Thank you again for the pleasure of taking part."

"Thank you that is amazing and quite accurate! The only part that is not really me is the line about being easily forgiving!!! Thanks again for the feedback and ability to see another very interesting form of intuitive reading. Thanks and best wishes."

"Thank you so much for your music interpretation. It is very accurate. Regarding the actual song, I really like it for the melody/sound rather than lyrics, and had not really thought much about the actual lyrics until I read them after I submitted the song to you, and then thought about how it was actually quite a sad song despite the happy sound, and I had never really experienced what the song was about. Oops... I then wondered how I would be 'read' but I think it's pretty much spot on. Once again, thank you for sharing your insights."

"Thank you for taking the time to reply and give me an insight into what you are doing. I cannot claim to understand all of what you are "saying," but my general impression is that you are a very generous person that seems to be at peace with yourself, or at least you seem to know in which direction you are heading to achieve that peace. All the very best with your book, whatever you follow…if the underlying message is love, compassion and understanding, then I think you're on the right track."

"It isn't often I say that someone knows me better than myself but obviously you do! Your interpretation of my song was so insightful, and in fact you pointed out things that were true about me that I hadn't thought of!!! Thank you so much for your thoughts - you made my day. Anyone will come away with a new perspective from this book."

CONTENTS

CHAPTER ONE

Introduction

We are all touched by music. Music connects us. We join together and share our favorite songs. We feel a sense of belonging with each other. Music enlivens us and it brings us joy and it brings us solace. We all have favorite songs which transport us in time and take us once again to experience those special moments. Music heals broken hearts. We share, we dance, we cry, we love and we make love to music. There is no barrier with music. Music can be the conduit that connects common man to his spirit. Music connects us to our inner voice. We are all equal under the Lord of Music.

Many of us yearn to find out about ourselves on a deeper level, and this unique guide will help you discover the secret messages and hidden meanings held within your favorite songs. Read My Song, Read My Heart, Read My Soul will help you learn about yourself on a more intuitive and accepting level and help you live the joyous and fulfilling life you desire. It is a bridge to help you connect with your inner self, your truth. This is a highly intuitive and abstract process. I hope that these Song Reads give you guidance and clarity, and help you understand the underlying meaning of your life and trust in your specialness.

Music allows the listener a freedom of imagination, interpretation and emotional response. Music touches each of us differently, but the unifying theme I have found is that these songs enable the listener to connect with Source. I like to use the word Source, but it is inter-changeable with The Divine, God or any words you choose to ascribe to this higher power. And just as there are many different religions and avenues of spirituality to connect with Source, there also seems to be a multitude of different sounds in music to connect with Source. Our favorite songs in some subtle way bring each of us to heaven. The underlying issue of virtually all the Song Reads I intuit have a sense of spiritual connection. This may not be the case for someone else who desires to try my methodology, but my clients seem to be attracted to me subconsciously for this reason. The beauty about this work is meeting wonderful people. They come and present themselves with their hearts open, vulnerable, sharing, ready for new experiences, con-fident and compassionate. It is a blessing and joy for me to connect with people so intimately.

I hope this book encourages you to be curious and look into the se-cret messages held in your favorite song. Look through the contents page of this book and locate your favorite song. If it does not appear in the list then see if you can locate your favorite band or musician. Turn straight to that particular Song Read and see if the Song Read applies to you as well. It can also be fun to locate songs and bands whose music you used to like in earlier years. Do you recognize an earlier version of yourself in this Song Read? Are your friends', sib-lings' or partner's favorite songs here? Then why not discover these Song Reads together? In fact, all of these Song Reads will on some level be relevant for everyone, as we are all connected, and what is in me is in you as well. If your favorite song does not appear in this book then why not contact me personally to receive a personalized Song Read? And also you won't have to wait too long until volume II of Read My Song, Read My Heart, Read My Soul is released!

Many people have asked me why I am so passionate about working with the secret messages in songs and how I discovered the intuitive tool of Song Reads. So maybe a little brief history is in order. I grew up in a middle-class Irish family, living in England. Looking back I can now see that as a little girl I was very sensitive to seeing spirits, sensing invisible things, hearing invisible things. In my adult years, episodes of precognition commenced and I started to see events happening in present time, but on the other side of the world and in advance. These experiences became normal to me, but I noticed that other people were not seeing the same things. I loved the invisible world but I didn't have an avenue to share these visions and so, on the whole, I felt quite odd and I was also secretly fearful that I was a touch crazy!

I am not a musician. In fact, I come from a large academic family and, although my five siblings and I did well at school, and were expected to study diligently and pass our exams, music was the one subject we were allowed to fail—and so we all did!

You will notice as you read through this book that I had not heard many of the songs before. I seem to be a bit of a fresh-faced baby with music. My iPod contains 25 chants and 25 "chill" tracks, so I exist with a very narrow repertoire of songs. The benefit of this is that, in the context of Read My Song, Read My Heart, Read My Soul, I interpret the hidden messages in your favorite music with no prior attachments. I come to your song blind, as such.

When I look back over the years, I can now see that my quest to interpret songs and music has played a pivotal theme in my life. If I had my time over, I would choose to study modern dance. I love how dancers interpret music. Dance is my favorite art form and, along with sculpture, has the capacity to move me through time, space, and dimensions.

Music first appeared for me at the age of twelve when I discovered my fifth favorite song, "Dreams" by Fleetwood Mac. My brother brought the record home from a holiday in America, and I used to sneak into his bedroom and listen to this track…repeatedly. I listened to it so much I scratched his LP!

In the old days, while listening to records, I loved the sounds within music, but lyrics were not important for me. So I was amazed as a student when a lyric became significant to me. I didn't realize it at the time but I had discovered my favorite lyric, which tellingly refers to the concepts of sounds, from the song "State of Independence" by Jon Anderson and Vangalis.

Another fundamental event occurred while I was an art student. I remember lying on a sofa, sobbing after I discovered the artist Kandinsky. I was drawn to and loved this artist's work, and as I delved into his history, I remember feeling very distressed at the discovery that his painting was based on interpreting music. Kandinsky had an insightful understanding of the affinities between painting and music, and he had been expressing and painting this since before I was born. I was distraught; I thought that this was my mission, to express music through art! I thought that this was my job in life. I cried for weeks. I'd lost my direction! Little did I know that music would manifest in my life, but in a different way. And, because of my haste, I did not discover that Kandinsky was also intrigued by the spiritual in art by seeing the invisible. Oh, why was I racing, why didn't I stay a little longer? Little did I know, but in the years to come the spiritual and the invisible would also become significant in my own life.

The initial inspiration for this book, Read My Song, Read My Heart, Read My Soul started with my quest to find the three songs which I wanted to be played at my funeral. I am not sure why this was so important for me. I had the sense that maybe I hadn't expressed myself fully and these songs would be my final chance to express who I was! I went to great lengths with this—a bit like a wedding, I guess. I was determined to get it right! My favorite two songs were apparent to me and the reasons why I liked them were also evident to me. The third song however was much more difficult to decide upon: I was caught between two songs, the song I thought I should pick and the song which had been with me for decades. After much contemplation, deliberation and angst, I realized that the song I thought I should pick was my ego talking. I wanted to pick this song because it said something about me and my values. Yet the remaining song talked from within me. It talked more of my essence and so this song was very easily settled upon.

Back then I pictured my funeral as a sombre affair with much wailing, crying and tissues! I visioned a lot of heartbreak! My funeral will probably be the only time I walk or am carried up the aisle, as I have never been married. So here I am being carried up the aisle in a tiny miniature coffin containing a few bones, as I intend to donate my organs, tissues and any other body parts to help save lives and to hopefully help science. From this quest to find my funeral songs I finally grasped that it was probably time to start expressing myself fully right now. Why the reticence? What was I so afraid of? Why was I hiding my light? I came to understand that if these songs help to express me then maybe it is the same for other people. Maybe favorite songs fully express hidden messages for all of us about ourselves.

So I began to study songs, and looked for guidance within my favorite song. Let me explain. In 2008 I came to a stage in life where I realized that I wasn't totally happy. On the surface I looked happy and I was living a "successful" life; I had a perfect partner, I had two fabulous, wonderful, brilliant children, I had a very successful business. I was living the life I thought I was supposed to live. However, something was wrong and something had been wrong for a long time. I didn't know what it was, but I was acutely aware that something was wrong. I had previously visited a psychoanalyst for a while, but with a few exceptions, hadn't come out much wiser. And something was still very wrong. So in 2008 I reached the decision that I wasn't doing life very well. My way wasn't working. It was time to give up my way of doing life and change. And I had no idea at all of what the change would be. Little did I know, but I had surrendered.

The following day, I felt guided to listen to my favorite song. I had liked this song for many years. The sound made me feel really, really big. I could drown in this sound. I felt inspired, joyful and endless. But I had never paid any attention to the lyrics. So for the first time I focused on the lyrics. My favorite song is "This is the Sea" by The

Waterboys and written by Mike Scott. As a summary, for me, the lyrics convey moving into the spiritual life. At the time I didn't know what spiritual meant. Spirituality, Religion, Spirit, Holy Spirit, Holy Ghost, Soul, Higher Self, The Divine. I didn't have a clue what any of this meant. So I patiently waited and pondered and prepared myself to receive any guidance as to how I would start my spiritual journey—and within a week or so my spiritual teacher arrived! Synchronicity was at play. I remember sitting down for my first spiritual class, and in the afternoon the word "home" appeared clairvoyantly to me three times. The word seemed to float down in front of the white board. I had arrived home! I started to breathe again. My favorite song had guided me home! Home for me is the spiritual life. My favorite song had guided me well.

I decided to write this book while having a telephone conversation with a close friend. At the time, my friend was experiencing enormous challenges in his life. While my friend was pouring his heart out to me, I felt guided, out of the blue, to ask him what his favorite song was. And, out of the blue, I was able to give him guidance and provide reassurance based on his favorite song! We were both amazed. I remember joking that I might write a book about secret messages held within songs. Little did I know, I had discovered my gift!

When I become quiet and ask why I feel drawn to interpreting the hidden massages in your favorite songs, I encounter the great dichotomy that speaks to me of The Divine Plan. Initially our favorite songs tell us about ourselves. They show us our differences, skills and talents, our specialness. Our favorite songs provide us with a golden nugget; a special talent, a special viewpoint, a special behavior, a special inflection. I sense that it is our responsibility to show, teach and shine with these golden nuggets. Being willing to "show and tell" and being patient to let others "practice and emulate." I perceive the opposite of this is also happening at the same time. These Song Reads also show us how connected we are. We connect and identify with our favorite songs. I sense that these Song Reads would apply for any two or more people liking the same song, as a song seems to serve as a sharing of qualities and behavior between people. I think that individual Song Reads would also apply, to a high degree, with people appreciating and liking the same band or musician. We seem to have lost sight of our essential interrelatedness. We understand the theory in the concept of unity, but Song Reads are a new way to illustrate this unity. People come together in unity when they connect to the same song. My motivations for these Song Reads are to provide guidance and to show us how connected we truly are. In the world of spirit we are all one. I am clear and hopeful about the role this work can play in the creation of a more beautiful world.

And for the Song Read skeptics out there! When I become quiet and ask, why am I working with the "good" news from our favorite songs and not the "bad" news from our favorite arguments, I receive the answer that the lesson is to develop compassion. If we like ourselves more, we can see more of that in ourselves and appreciate more of the qualities we like in others. We are then open to developing compassion and to understanding our weaknesses. Maybe we don't love ourselves enough yet. As in, I love me and so I love you. Possibly only after this has occurred are we finally able to deal with the aspects of ourselves which we consider to be negative.

These Song Reads are intuitive and abstract due to the nature of the lyrics, the nature of the music and the nature of the individual person. Music has both a descriptive and an abstract quality. The method I use to intuit these Song Reads for you is simple. My client is not present for the Song Read. Even though I am based in Australia, my clients come from all over the world from places far away such as America, England, and Singapore. I correspond with my clients over the Internet. My client is not present, but they have provided me with three clues: their Christian name, their favorite song and the musician who performs the song. I try to keep it simple!

I meditate for an extended period so that my energy field is clear and so I can receive accurate guidance. I perceive and sense the energy body of my client and the energy field of my client's favorite song. I listen to their favorite song and I ask my guides, (ascended masters, teachers and angels) to interpret the hidden messages in their favorite songs and to pass this information through me as a channel. I trust and allow the energy from my guides to flow through me. I try to receive the secret messages rather than go looking for them. I voice record the Song Read; the sensations, vibrations and messages I receive. I record the information as it arrives. The music in their favorite song produces a feeling in me. The instruments, style of voice and lyrics have an impact on me and my energy field.

Sometimes the music helps to define you and sometimes your soul and subconscious are speaking through the music to you. In many cases, we are interpreting the sound of music! These Song Reads are not essays. The Song Reads tend to start and stop and repeat themselves as I receive guidance of the hidden messages for you.

Remember, we all have free will. You have free will to change your mind about things and to change the way you think. So if you don't like an aspect of a Song Read, my advice to you is to choose to let it go and don't put your focus on that area. Take what you like and leave the rest!

In addition, these Song Reads are not the only or full version of you. We all have contradictions within us. A song, by its nature, will not cover all aspects of you, but it will tend to highlight some important themes for you or about you. This is not a full birth/personality read of you. My hunch is that your favorite three songs will give a very significant intuitive read of your profile and your favorite 12 songs will give a full intuitive read of you, your personality, preferences and psyche.

I have changed all of the names of my clients for these Song Reads to protect their privacy and I offer my very special thanks to all these pioneers for generously offering these songs to me with openness. I feel that all of these Song Reads are "good," and as we are all connected they are all relevant and ultimately helpful for everyone.

So there you have it. I hope this helps to explain my process. I trust you enjoy perusing this book just as much as I did writing it. I hope you see and recognize yourself, with joy, in your favorite songs.

Uncommon terms are defined throughout this book as they are introduced. If you need a quick reference or a word is unclear, please visit my blog, readmysongreadmysoul.com for a great glossary and other resources.

And if you are walking down the street one day, passing a church, and you hear these three songs: "This is the Sea" by The Waterboys, "Rockin' Gypsies" by Willie and Lobo and "State of Independence" by Jon and Vangelis, I have probably passed over. Please come into the church, pay your respects and leave a donation for the priest.

Love,

Awen

CHAPTER TWO

"Alison" performed by Elvis Costello

If this is your favorite song, then you are probably special in these ways:

- Romantic
- Possess a giving nature
- Heart-centered
- Refined
- Sensitive
- Reflective
- Creative
- Truthful and honest
- Sincere
- Appreciate black humor
- A little bit different
- Comfortable with emotions

Client: Jonah

It has been a pleasure to intuit this Song Read for you.

I interpret your deeper connection to the song in this way:

This is a sad song at the beginning and has a sad sound. You are a romantic and get heavily involved in your relationships. Is the song autobiographical for you? You are a sweet tender soul, romantic and gentle. You have a beautiful heart. You have a beautiful heart that wants to share. You are generous. You have a wonderful, generous heart. Your energy field tingles with generosity. You are generous in your thoughts, although not necessarily materialistically generous. You are generous in your thoughts and in consideration for others. This is how you are generous. You have a soft sweet personality. As I am intuiting this Song Read I am aware that we haven't really left your heart. Other music and songs will express different aspects of you. This song very much activates your heart center.

You are refined, sensitive, reflective and creative. You are at home with abstraction and creativity. You probably have refined taste buds as well. This music brings out your finer qualities.

Possibly there is some hurt here. The sound seems to wrap you up, as in a warm, comforting blanket.

What a wonderful open heart!

I sense that your purpose and wishes are faithful to your inner values. You try to make the best possible choice that you are able to make. Truth is important to you. These lyrics have probably happened to you, perhaps a loss of security, or rejection. There is some real sadness here in these lyrics for you. There is a sense of a loss here. You connect emotionally to these lyrics and the sadness.

You are sincere and romantic. You also seem to have a rather black sense of humor. There is a lot of happiness in you too. You also appear to be idiosyncratic. You are a little bit different.

Ballads suit you. The energy goes down into your arms, which are an extension of your heart chakra. There is some "country" in you too, as in respect for country values.

You are very sincere, unguarded and honest.

The energy of the Hindu Sanskrit word "Namaste" (which means I honor your divinity) suits you. I sense that you naturally honor the divinity in others. And I, in turn, also honor the divinity in you. Namaste.

Client Feedback

"That all makes me sound so wonderful, I'm not sure you are talking about me. I'm really not that nice. LOL. But aspects of it are certainly true. Ballads do suit me. Music (as in listening) has always been big in my life, and finding an absolute favorite amongst many is near impossible. "Alison" has always been one of them."

Jonah

CHAPTER THREE

"Baker Street" performed by Gerry Rafferty

If this is your favorite song, then you are probably special in these ways:

* Aware of spiritual realms
* A big personality
* Possess high energy
* Have a good sense of humor
* Intellectual
* Willing to look inward
* Insightful and Aware
* Profound
* Gentle
* Open to accurate intuition and inner knowing
* A Powerful personality
* A storyteller

Client: Courtney

It has been an absolute treat to intuit this Song Read for you. What a wonderful song and sound!

I interpret the hidden messages in your favorite song in this way:

You like this song. It connects you with London! You are laughing. You have a big laugh. The saxophone pulls and raises you up, connecting you and your energy field to "All that is."

You especially like the sax because it has a big sound and this reflects you. You have a big energy field. You are big in both personality and energy. You also have a good sense of humor. Your humor lights up like fireworks. You thoroughly enjoy a deep laugh! You love the saxophone and your connection seems to be with the intelligent aspect of the sax. The sound transports you to Source.

It seems that the beginning part of this song is autobiographical for you. You connect to the lyrics. Perhaps you have a tendency at times to delay gratification. "Shedding tears, attempting, delaying," and sometimes not paying attention to the big picture, and getting caught up in the little details of life. I sense this is the autobiographical element for you—sometimes ignoring the signs presented to you, and racing ahead and occasionally not taking the time to smell the roses. You possibly have quite a busy life.

You are a very intellectual individual, and at times your intellectual focus can overtake your emotional responses. You may experience a touch of pain expressing love, even when you feel it strongly. This saxophone vibration helps you to express love.

You have a willingness to look inward. You are very aware when things are not going right in your life. You like and connect easily to the gentle melody. The lyrics are more searching and profound while the music quality is gentler—a paradox which you also express. Gentle music running behind everything happening in your life. There is gentleness and an easy sway, which is overlapped with insight, which makes you very aware. The gentleness of the melody in the background is the hint to *tune in* to your intuition and inner knowing. I sense that this is the guidance held within this song for you.

It is important for you that people have soul. Perhaps this is what you are really looking for, an expression of our souls. For you "home" can have many meanings: "home" as in a house, "home" as in your country, "home" as in friends, and "home" as in relationships. But with the sound of the saxophone, it seems that we are really talking about "home" as in The Divine.

And here come the fireworks, expressed for you through the electric guitar. Maybe you also express fireworks at times! These instruments invite you to come out of your head space and to connect through your heart space. You trust the sound you are hearing and let the sound take you where it will.

The saxophone is obviously the power in this music. The feeling you have when you listen to the sax is the feeling of your own power.

The lyrics are presented in a storytelling format. The singer on one level is telling a story about mundane life in London, but on another level, he is telling a story about how we miss our own signs. We ignore them. Again a paradox—the everyday mundane way we travel through life, paying attention to the details of our physical reality, but the motion of life is again the gentle melody running underneath the surface, which has a deeper essence of profound unity in our consciousness. You sometimes become aware of this, and then you easily transit into the great saxophone sounds of the universe. This is also seen in fairy tales and mythology.

You are a storyteller too.

Client Feedback

"HiAwen,

Just had a quick read of your interpretation and I think it's very spot on. It's true on all fronts & levels. Very good. Funny coincidence, but at this moment, I have the lyrics for Baker Street on my desk & will look at them again."

Courtney

CHAPTER FOUR

"Belief" performed by John Mayer

If this is your favorite song, then you are probably special in these ways:

- Deep and complex
- Peaceful
- Open to intuition and invisible guidance
- See the big picture in life
- Possess a good sense of humor
- A deep and profound thinker
- Possess strong ethics and honor
- Intellectual
- A curious spirit
- Aware
- Idealistic
- A philosopher

Client: Ryan

It has been a pleasure to intuit this Song Read for you. I had not heard this music before.

I interpret your deeper connection to the song in this way:

You are a deep, complex individual. I have the sense that you would like to be able to fly. And you possibly have a belief in angels and unicorns. You are a peaceful soul and you also appear to have a wide, wide vision of life. You have very open viewpoints of life. Your vision seems to encompass much. Throughout this interpretation I have the image of a flying unicorn above the clouds. This seems to illustrate higher mind and the ability to see the big picture in life. You also have a good sense of humor, as I now see your unicorn is wearing sunglasses!

You like the lyrics and the connection for you is probably the lyrics more than the music. You are comfortable in the thinking realm. You possess good, strong ethics, and honor. Your strengths appear to be your intellect, your openness to inquiry and your vision. These qualities are very pronounced in you.

There may be some fuzziness with your emotions, possibly hurt and a sense of burden. There appears to be some emotional pain. Perhaps at times you do not stand up for yourself. Or maybe it is pain due to some misunderstanding, and you are unable to accept it when people unintentionally hurt you. Swallowing hurt is not helpful for you. However, it is also clear that you work really hard to integrate your emotional self, and I feel you are driven to do this because of your depth of awareness.

You are a deep thinker and a complex soul. There is perhaps some internal conflict within you.

Your emotions are now coming through. The beginning guitar sound and the beginning musical sounds of this song touch you. You are connected with Source. The music element appears to be exceedingly helpful for you, as it allows your emotions to be present. You probably find it far easier to express your intellectual and rational side than your emotional side. So music really is a great panacea for you. You connect to the musical element and this helps you to connect emotionally. And the musical element can allow you to become quite absorbed and lost and thus come out from behind your mental faculties. Your intellect is strong.

There is idealism to the lyrics and for you there is a great deal of truth to the lyrics too. We all have beliefs, but a belief does not mean it is the truth. We honor our beliefs and we support our beliefs but the question is, why? So there is a sense of the profound with the lyrics, and your thinking also tends to be profound. This idealism and this ability to penetrate through the excuse of belief to the hidden motivations in people is in you too. There is a philosopher in you.

CHAPTER FIVE

"Below my Feet" performed by Mumford and Sons

If this is your favorite song, then you are probably special in these ways:

- Appreciate magic
- Open to your emotions
- Feel deeply
- Aware of the darker side of life as well as the lighter side of life
- Have the ability to be still
- Possess empathy
- Complex
- Serious
- Compassionate
- Gentle
- Possess wholesome values
- Reflective and refined
- Insightful
- A teacher

Client: Brittany
It has been a pleasure to intuit this Song Read for you. I had not heard this music before.

I interpret your deeper connection to the song in this way:

There is some magic in this sound for you. There are some fairies here too. It seems that the gentle sound at the beginning of the song is the sound of pixies and fairies existing in elevated land forms, such as mountains. I think it is a fresh energy. It is a high, cold, clear, fresh energy.

The lyrics are significant to you. You are open to your emotions and you feel deeply. This song connects you to Spirit. You have probably suffered pain, like many of us. So you are aware of the darker side of life as well as the lighter side of life. When I am intuiting this Song Read for you, there is lot of stillness and quietness. There is some sadness from this pain. There is also some acceptance here for you. You have chosen to view your challenges as learning opportunities. You have a good deal of empathy for other people because of overcoming your own challenges. There is a little bit of energy blockage in your vision. You perhaps haven't seen everything clearly. There is possibly another side to this blockage, and it may be that the blinkers have kept you safe from seeing everything. This might have actually helped protect you. I think that you used to be angry but you are less so now. There is complexity in you and seriousness.

In a way the lyrics allude to the spiritual journey of being wounded and encountering the less desirable in our lives and overcoming this. We overcome this pain by choosing to learn from it. As we learn we change our perceptions. We forgive. Hopefully, we come out the other end with a sense of acceptance and gratitude. We always seem to gain the gift of compassion. Compassion halts judgment, and it is fairly clear that we could all probably do with more compassion in the world. This compassion is within you. It is possible that some of us are here to bring the healing essence of compassion to others. And with empathy we can do this, because we have gone through those fires ourselves. This may or may not be you, but you are aware of this healing dynamic. I sense this has happened to you. I sense that there is probably some biography here for you.

The outdoors and mountainous regions would almost certainly be good for you. I don't see snow. I see cold. I think you would enjoy the clarity and the energy. The cleanness. You would enjoy the cleanness of the energy where the land is high and elevated. You are a gentle soul and possess wholesome values. You perhaps enjoy poetry and you enjoy the poetry of these song lyrics too. You can be reflective and refined. You now have, though maybe at an earlier age you didn't, the gift of much deeper insight.

The lyrics have a spiritual component, suggesting individuals serving each other, rather than expressing blame and seeking victimhood when dealing with challenges. We can learn from these situations instead. This is a great message for everyone. We know we have arrived at a more enlightened state when we ask the question, "How may I serve?" rather than; "what's in it for me?" Maybe you feel this pull to some extent. So this song has a message to teach us and maybe this teacher is within you too.

CHAPTER SIX

"Bizarre Love Triangle" performed by New Order

If this is your favorite song, then you are probably special in these ways:

- Intellectual
- Kind
- Sensitive to the circumstance of others
- Compassionate
- Desire to help and care for other people
- Happy
- Logical and rational
- Responsible
- Diligent
- Loyal
- Possess a sharing nature
- A good friend and a good mother / nurturing parent

Client: Natasha

It has been a pleasure to intuit this Song Read for you.

I interpret your deeper connection to the song in this way:

The shape expressed in the title of this song appears to be you: Intellect, emotions and you.

You are intellectual and kind. You feel the beat energetically on your right-hand side which is your intellectual, rational side. In fact all of the music is playing on your right-hand side. You are an intellectual person. There is an interested, compassionate friend in you, who desires to help others. The music connects you to Source. There is a happy, delightful quality in you.

You tend to work and process using your thinking capacity rather than your emotions. You probably rely on your logical and rational explanations. You tend to sense interpretations of events, upsets and situations from this perspective. The message seems to be: trust your feelings. This may be daunting and uncomfortable at first, but your heart wants to be interpreted, understood and expressed through emotions, both the supposedly good ones and bad ones. All feelings are actually neutral, so maybe just allow these feelings to be. You suffer from worry at times, or maybe you pay too much attention to physical time or to holding on to old beliefs, even when they have outworn their usefulness. From time to time your logic may overtake your emotions, and you sometimes do not pay attention to your feelings. Your feelings seem to want an outlet, and if you desire more balance, acknowledging your feelings and processing your feelings will give you more internal harmony. By incorporating and working through your feelings, the anxiety, worry and confusion, which seem to come from choosing to employ logic and rationale habitually, will subside.

You fulfill your responsibilities and duties well. You apply yourself and work diligently at the various tasks in life. You are also loyal. It is possible that you do not receive the recognition or praise which your concern for others may warrant. But the message is to give attention, approval and appreciation to ourselves too. This is also connected with choosing to experiment with recognizing your feelings.

You possess a smiling, sharing nature and you truly care for your friends. You are a good friend and help people considerably. You like the xylophone sound. I almost see that you would enjoy dancing as if you had drumsticks in your hands. You enjoy moving your arms. Physical affection is good and nurturing for you. The combination of the beat and the guitar and other instruments is quite delightful to you and it helps to connect you to Source. You are happy when you listen to this song.

You express a very happy exterior. I sense that you would be a good mother too. You are an attractive person.

You are a kind soul and you care for others and you don't want to hurt others, but by paying attention to others you sometimes neglect your own inner confusion. Prayer and surrendering to a Source which is bigger than any of us could be key for you to achieve enhanced internal balance, if that is what you seek. You are perhaps running through life and maybe sense that there is something else. If this is the case, choose to ask and it will be shown to you.

Client Feedback

"Thank you so much for your music interpretation. It is very accurate. Regarding the actual song, I really like it for the melody/sound rather than lyrics, and had not really thought much about the actual lyrics until I read them after I submitted the song to you, and then thought about how it was actually quite a sad song despite the happy sound, and I had never really experienced what the song was about. Oops... I then wondered how I would be 'read' but I think it's pretty much spot on. Being a teenager in the 80s I do look to music of that era as being happy and simple; naïve too, and though I think New Order was probably a bit later than that, whenever I hear their music it always makes me feel happy.

Once again, thank you for sharing your insights."

Natasha

CHAPTER SEVEN

"Bohemian Rhapsody" performed by Queen

If this is your favorite song, then you are probably special in these ways:

- Imaginative
- Comfortable expressing and feeling emotions
- Enthusiastic
- Appreciate the grand and epic in scale
- Sometime enjoy chaos and confusion
- Possess faith
- Exciting and expansive
- Adventurous
- Creative
- Sexy
- Comfortable being in both relaxed and active states
- Open to intuition
- Intellectual
- Accepting of people and circumstances

Client: Luke

I thoroughly enjoyed intuiting this Song Read for you.

I interpret your deeper connection to the song in this way:

Your imagination, visions and fantasies are activated by this song. This song connects you with Spirit. I sense that you connect with this music through your emotions and you express and feel your emotions quite easily. This is healthy for you. You express your full range of emotions from love and joy to pain. You feel the energy of pain easily.

There seems to be a sense of a journey through life, a journey which all of us take, the highs and the lows, and you partake of this journey with relish and enthusiasm. You are open to the experiences encountered along the way.

Some of the musical elements connect you to Source very easily, the lament of the singing voice especially. The electric guitar and its sound sit very well in your energy field. However, there is also some hurt in your heart with this, which tends to manifests energetically in your left arm.

You enjoy the fusion, the sense of epic and the touch of chaos within this sound. The fast sections run through your energy and expel very quickly through your energy field. With you, there seems to be an element of faith which comes through the operetta. You are an exciting individual. You are open to adventure, open to creativity and open to expressing yourself. You possess sex appeal too. I almost sense that you want to wring out every drop of emotion, expression and learning from your experiences. You are comfortable in both a relaxed state and in a very active state. You have openness to faith, which allows you to just be.

Sometimes there may be confusion. Almost too much expansion for you to handle, though you handle expansion well. So my sense for you is the whole epic, the whole operatic quality of this huge, huge song is what you connect to, and you like to have these qualities and drama in your life because they make you feel alive.

Possibly the lyrics will be secondary for you. You are very open to your intuition. You are open to your intellect and emotions as well. You present as quite balanced in this way. I feel that you perhaps appreciate the darkness, the pure raw emotion. This allows you to feel alive. Interestingly the sound which resonates with you is the "ooo" sound from the singer's voice. In the Tarot the zero represents both "The Fool" and "Spiritual Enlightenment." When something happens three times, as in the triple o, it means that there is a spiritual connection. It is The Divine talking to you.

Sometimes there is a little bit of bewilderment with your thinking. Possibly too much expansion and perhaps some concepts which are much too big for you to grasp. You will, however, grow into this expanded state, because every time we return to concepts we discover new things. I sense that you are very creative, very open to new experiences. You receive from these lyrics the emotional experience you crave. I do not see a lot of judgment in you. I see the reverse. I see acceptance in you. You accept the various paths, incidents and events which happen to you in your life and you glean meaning from these. You are always looking for life in all of these circumstances. You are very highly aware, perhaps subconsciously, of "the illusion" down here on planet Earth.

CHAPTER EIGHT

"Born to Run" performed by Bruce Springsteen

If this is your favorite song, then you are probably special in these ways:

- Have an abundant source of energy
- Possess a good sense of humor
- Sincere
- Stand up for yourself
- Confident and have conviction
- Follow your goals and are results-orientated
- Prepared to take risks
- Open to guidance
- Happy in relationships
- Logical
- Take initiative
- Have a warm nature

Client: Patrick

It has been a pleasure to intuit this Song Read for you.

I interpret your deeper connection to the song in this way:

You love the sound, the great joyous rhapsody of sound at the beginning. You enjoy the energy of the music, expressed through the guitars and the triangle at the beginning of this song. The percussion instruments—triangle, bell, xylophone and others—have an effect on your energy field. This music connects you to Source. You love the guitar. You appreciate the energy of this music. And you are a person who has an abundant source of energy.

You also have a solid sense of humor. I perceive that you enjoy having a good time. You are quite masculine. You are sincere, you are not fearful to back down from an argument and you are not fearful to ask the question "why?"

You have a lot of energy. You may even look or dress a bit like this singer. You possess confidence. You seem to be sure of yourself, and you have the confidence and conviction to stand up for what you believe in. You are happy to follow your dreams. You are confident to make decisions and to follow your goals.

You seem to understand yourself quite well, and this is to your advantage. You are prepared to take risks. You are open to guidance, which you usually feel as a gut sensation. You are happy in relationships, and your manner and your personality appear to be masculine. You likely have a logical mind, display initiative and are results-orientated. You are also warm. You perhaps have some reticence expressing emotions and prefer to mask any hurt you feel.

You enjoy these lyrics. You enjoy how they "strum in the car." The lyrics may have meaning for you. I sense you are somebody who really wants to experience life. You rush to experience life. You like to experience a sense of freedom.

It is important for you to not let others take your energy from you. Sometimes people can suck your energy from you. It is good for you to keep this energy for yourself. So the message is to maintain your energy, first by becoming aware of how your energy feels, and then by being conscious of people not taking this from you. Sometimes your energy can deplete and you perhaps do not know why. It is possible that you give too easily and put others ahead of your own needs.

So, it can be helpful to take better care of your boundaries

CHAPTER NINE

"Champagne Supernova" performed by Oasis

If this is your favorite song, then you are probably special in these ways:

- Gentle
- Passionate
- Open to emotions and feel deeply
- Dramatic
- Warm-hearted
- Intellectual
- Sensitive
- Value the specialness in people and yourself
- Aware of the spiritual realm
- Looking for transformation
- Curious
- Interested in The Collective (Unity Consciousness)
- May well be a magnetic personality too

Client: Harry

It has been a pleasure to intuit this Song Read for you.

I interpret your deeper connection to the song in this way:

The sound of the water lapping along the shoreline and the sound of the guitar connects you to Source. So you are connected before the lyrics have even started. You are gentle, passionate, open to your emotions and feel deeply. I sense some drama in you. This song connects you to Source very easily. You are warm-hearted and have a big heart. You are intellectual and you are sensitive, but hide this sensitivity under your mask to some extent.

You sense the specialness of yourself, but not exclusively. You perceive that everyone has special talents and skills. And you, like many of us, do not necessarily express your talents. And you probably know this. The Collins Australian Dictionary definition of "supernova" is: "A star that explodes and for a few days becomes one hundred million times brighter than the sun." This is a beautiful definition. What does this mean for you?

This song easily connects you. Your arms are raised and outwards. It brings you up to The Divine. You want to connect and join in the choir. The choir is the choir of the mass population, (The collective Consciousness.) You like feeling deeply and you like feeling the full range of your emotions. It helps to make you feel alive. This is the drama element within you. This also means that you will, at times, choose to enter into more painful emotions, because you want to explore and experience these, too.

You sense the spirit world, but don't necessarily arrive there as much as you would like to. But this awareness is apparent within you. I have received the words, "Hanging out to dry." Have you maybe at times drunk too much? Or meddled with drugs a bit too much? If you have, this may have been so that you could escape from this physical world and connect to other realms.

It appears that you are looking for some transformation. The lyrics can be quite cryptic, and so they are going to have a special meaning for you. Maybe you have played the victim role and it is now time to take responsibility for you and your own actions. You are curious. You seem to be questioning "why." Your questioning seems to be concerned with the theme of "what life is about." These lyrics have special meaning for you, and if you can uncover the emotion or visualize the story here, it will be a key for you. There is a strong possibility that this is the key; a transformation.

You love the instrumental sound. It resembles the sound of the Collective, and this draws you into the song. So the music seems to be what is pulling at you, magnetizing you, especially the rousing aspect of the music. The instrumental holds for you a sense of everyone rising up together. This music can transport you. You enjoy the pleasures of the physical realm, but you are also aware of the spiritual realm.

The lyrics look back at the past but there is also a secret allusion to the future—if we choose to change and transform.

I wish you all the best and I wish you many blessings from heaven!

Client Feedback

"Thank you for your reply, you are accurate in what your music reading has uncovered, I never thought so many things could be uncovered by a song, although I adore my music and different songs generate different emotions and levels of happiness or sadness for me, so it makes sense that we connect with lyrics and instrumental music, thanks."

Harry

CHAPTER TEN

"Clocks" performed by Coldplay

If this is your favorite song, then you are probably special in these ways:

- Open to emotions and feelings
- Intuitive
- Joyful
- Possess depth in your personality
- Passionate
- Hopeful
- Have faith
- Drawn to a sense of awe and wonder
- Believe in miracles and magic
- Searching, maybe not consciously, for the spirit within
- Aware of the home of spirit and higher self
- Expectant and optimistic

Client: Julian

It has been a pleasure to intuit this Song Read for you.

I interpret your deeper connection to the song in this way:

The sound of this music stirs you and rouses you. It helps to connect you to Source. You feel very easily and are very open to your emotions and intuition. You express joy, depth and passion. The piano keys hold significance for you and help to lift you to another dimension. This song connects you to Spirit. The sound lifts you up and gives you hope, faith, a sense of awe, a sense of wonder, a sense of miracles and a sense of magic. This is what the piano keys seem to symbolize for you, particularly the higher notes. There is also a searching quality within you.

There has probably been some struggle for you in life. There appears to be some blurred communication, or rigidity and holding onto old habits and beliefs, even when they have outlived their usefulness. Many of us have clarity issues with communication, not listening fully and attentively, difficulties speaking clearly, and also difficulties speaking from the heart. Sometimes you may experience difficulties with the free flow of information between your head and your heart.

The sound helps you fly. I think of an airplane flying. And this sound, more than anything else in the whole song, allows you to fly, a bit like Superman! But more similar to an airplane. There is some speed, some sense of urgency, and I perceive that you can't quite keep up with the pace. It may be beneficial for you to slow down a bit. The airplane image is the fullest energy image here. The airplane takes you home. To the home of spirit, to the home of your higher self. And I sense urgency, a feeling of chaos and haste to arrive home within yourself.

The piano is very joyful for you. Your arms out held out wide at your sides. You are expressing "movements in joy."

This song seems to allude to the spirit within you. It is your internal sense of monadic self (the spiritual life atom of The Divine). Your spirit, your soul. It is likely that you will find your greatest security in your soul. Not somewhere external. For you it appears to be internal.

Consider the famous spiritual mantra "I am that I am." We are everything. Sometimes nothing else compares to this great sense of understanding, that we are everything! "I am that I am." Terrific!

There is expectancy in you, a twirling sensation. Twirling and spirit seem to go together. You are expectant, optimistic, and have a surety of belief, you are very sure. So this music is deeply about you, your connection to spirit, and your connection to your sense of the internal you. This can be a great spiritual song. The lyrics are quite poetic and this may also be what attracts you. The lyrics are very clear and expressive.

Blessings to you.

CHAPTER ELEVEN

"Come Around" performed by Mental as Anything

If this is your favorite song, then you are probably special in these ways:

- A happy soul
- Have an open, easy energy field
- Considerate and caring
- Balanced with intellect and emotions
- Have positive self-possession
- Respectful
- Accept yourself and others
- In the flow of giving and receiving
- Affectionate
- A Counselor, Healer and Teacher
- Helpful
- Genuinely like people
- Nurture yourself and your own needs in a positive way
- Forgive others easily

Client: Sophie
It has been a pleasure to intuit this Song Read for you. I had not heard this music before.

I interpret your deeper connection to the song in this way:

The techno sound connects you to Source. You are a happy soul. You have an open, easy energy field. You care for others easily and possess a good and healthy balance between your intellect and emotions. You have a positive self-possession. You respect and accept yourself and others.

Your crown chakra is very open and connected to The Divine. You have an easy flow of energy. You demonstrate an easy flow of giving and receiving. You are affectionate and enjoy hugging and holding people. It is highly likely that people go to you for counsel. You offer good, fair, helpful, unbiased advice to your friends. You are the mainstay of a group. You are a helpful soul and contribute to the welfare of others. You have the ability to heal and teach. People learn by observing your behavior.

You genuinely like people and people like you in return. You are accepting of others. You are considerate and caring. You also look after yourself and your own needs too, so you are not a needy person. You are open to new people, open to new experiences. You have a very clean and open energy field. You are open to new ideas and new viewpoints. You forgive others easily as well.

The only minor problem which may surface is that maybe you are over-organized at times, or can be a touch critical with detail. But you have within you the remedy for this.

You are a happy soul, both connected and grounded. You smile and share easily.

Client Feedback

"Thank you that is amazing and quite accurate! The only part that is not really me is the line about being easily forgiving!!! Thanks again for the feedback and ability to see another very interesting form of intuitive reading. Thanks and best wishes."

Sophie

CHAPTER TWELVE

"Comfortably Numb" performed by Pink Floyd

If this is your favorite song, then you are probably special in these ways:

- Aware of the spiritual realm
- A profound individual
- Possess deep thought and deep understanding
- Have a yearning desire for…
- A loner
- Believe in miracles
- Passionate
- Like to relax
- Magnetic
- Sexy
- Mysterious
- Imposing

Client: Guy

It has been a pleasure to intuit this Song Read for you.

I interpret your deeper connection to the song in this way:

You seem to be wondering what the world is about. There is pain here, too. You have an understanding of the reality beyond the horizon, of what is real. At times you possibly experience the confusion of being down here on planet Earth. This happens with a few people, this sense of "Why am I down here?" You are a profound individual with deep thought and deep understanding. There is a sense of longing within you in the musical interlude. You are reaching for what you know to be there but it is eluding you. And that is sad for you. Many of us resort to drugs, alcohol and cigarettes to anesthetize this understanding. This is almost one of those, "dark night of the soul" experiences—the longing for the peace and bliss of what our heart tells us is possible. (Interestingly the words "peace" and "bliss" actually appear as "beace" and "pliss," which seems to give some indication of the confusion.) It is likely that this has been occurring to you since childhood, since your teenage years.

You are probably a bit of a loner, but not lonely. You have access to people when you need them.

It is interesting, because I know it comes from the album, but I do get the sense of somebody literally walking into a wall repeatedly. There could even be the sense that at a higher vibration it is possible to actually walk through the wall, as in miracles. You probably do believe in miracles and would welcome their appearance in your life.

This is a secret part of your personality. You may benefit from having a few more intimate, soulful, deep companions to share and express the passion, the longing, the depth of you. It is to your advantage to settle down with somebody who understands you deeply. And, by sharing this side of yourself, it will free you to quite a large extent.

A helpful verb for you to consider is "To glance." When you glance at something and it arouses your interest, if you focus upon it, it will by its nature expand and manifest into a vision for you.

You like to relax and would probably enjoy yoga or a yoga relaxation audio CD.

This song encompasses many musical interludes which become deep and passionate, and this represents the depth and passion in you.

And the high notes, this is your longing—your attempts and striving to arrive beyond the physical horizon. What a wonderful choice of music! The challenge is, of course, to not be comfortably numb, and you aren't. You will strive until you find what you are looking for.

There is great depth here. There seems to be some sense of autobiography for you too. There are other ways to experience grand blissful visions, such as when we are connected to The Divine. Being connected to The Divine through meditation can be a more healthful way, as this path doesn't destroy us and we still experience peace and bliss.

You feel deeply and I imagine somebody with dark hair. Your depth makes it quite easy for you to be magnetic to others and you use this to attract people to some degree. I think you must be quite a sexy person. Magnetic and sexy and I think the girls (or the boys) would find you a bit of mystery. Your magnetism is very big, you have a lot of presence, but you are probably aware of this. You are imposing, but in a nice way. People look up to you and some people are secretly envious of you. You possess many classic Scorpio qualities, such as magnetism, mystery, sex appeal and passion.

I've enjoyed listening to the passion here. I wish you love, support, relaxation, truth. But above all else, I wish you being you!

CHAPTER THIRTEEN

"Dear Prudence" performed by Doug Parkinson

If this is your favorite song, then you are probably special in these ways:

- Expectant
- Drawn to a sense of awe
- Deep and passionate
- Feel freely
- Honest
- Decent
- Loyal
- A happy person
- Enjoy being with your friends
- Sensitive to the connectedness between nature, animals and humans
- Value beauty
- See the big vision of life

Client: Bella

I have thoroughly enjoyed intuiting this Song Read for you.

I interpret your deeper connection to the song in this way:

These are the images which present themselves through the guitar riff at the beginning of the music: wide-eyed, open, expectant, and a sense of awe. You are a deep and passionate individual who feels freely. You are honest, decent and loyal, and an open individual with a big smiley face! You are a happy person who enjoys being with your friends.

Probably the lyrics mean more to you than the music. The lyrics are the message. The message seems to be the connection between people, nature and animals, understanding that we are all connected.

The rousing aspect of the music moves you, and it helps you to connect to a bigger life (and a bigger love) than an individual human life.

You may sometimes feel defensive. You are probably reticent to express your inner vision, and the beauty of the world around you, your deep understanding of connectedness between nature, animals and humans. There may be some hurt in your heart. The hurt seems to be an old emotional hurt.

The lyrics...tell me you like beauty, you admire beauty, you are open to beauty and you also value the beauty of nature. Beauty is a characteristic of our soul. When we open our eyes, we can also choose to open up clairvoyantly and to see far more than what is physically there in front of us. The message for you seems to be the spiritual reality of "We are a part of everything and all is connected." In addition, the message reminds you to go into your ajna chakra and to see the big vision of life, which you are very well able to do. Maybe you do sometimes become mired in the details, but this music is a gentle reminder for you to ascend into your bigger vision. You have access to this enhanced and expanded "big picture" vista. Taking this step will help you to accept all aspects of life and all aspects of behavior.

The reference to the child may be to the spiritual inner child within all of us. This inner child is connected with our soul far more than our adult self is. Our inner child is more straightforward and honest, and our inner child enjoys fun and spontaneity. This is part of our creativity, and it is important to have this in our life along with the balance of work, responsibility and maturity. I sense that in this song the lead female is you. She is your inner child, and the music reminds you to live the gifts of your inner child. Children are easily connected with nature, elements of nature, fairies and animals. As a child, you probably enjoyed being outside, twirling with your arms open, taking everything in and understanding that everything is part of the whole. The sky has no boundaries, it is limitless; the sun is the giver of life. The child enjoys play and experiences joy. And a child views obstacles—which seem to be represented for you as clouds—kindly. The message appear to be: live and embrace your inner child, and view life from the highest and biggest vision possible.

Enjoy the beauty of nature. Enjoy the gift of each brand new day.

CHAPTER FOURTEEN

"Déjà Vu" performed by Crosby, Stills, Nash and Young

If this is your favorite song, then you are probably special in these ways:

- Insightful
- Gentle
- Sincere
- Have a good sense of humor
- Open to emotions
- Express yourself clearly
- Enjoy mystery and discovery
- Sensitive to other dimensions and worlds
- Intellectual
- Accomplished
- Initiate projects
- Possess a warm and expansive personality
- Have a refined mind which looks beneath the surface
- An illustrator (e.g. illustrate a picture or a point of view)

Client: William

Thank you for the opportunity to intuit this Song Read for you. I had not heard this music before. These sounds are a real treat! This inter-

pretation is quite abstract in places and I feel drawn to deliberately
keep it so.

I interpret your deeper connection to the song in this way:

I am sensing the sound of tambourines in you. And the sound of a
rice shaker seems to express you too. You are comfortable sitting
around in a circle with close friends.

You are insightful. You appreciate the acoustic in life. You are
happy in intimate situations. You are gentle, very sincere and have a
good sense of humor. This song connects you to Source throughout
your energy field and right down to your legs.

You are happy in the world of emotions and you express yourself
clearly. You also like mystery, and you are aware of other dimensions
and worlds. You enjoy unraveling intricacies.

This song is brilliant in your energy field. It particularly lights up
your right-hand side. Your intellect and sense of discovery is strong.
Your thoughts are lucid.

Your energy body is presenting very brightly on one side. You display a yang masculine energy. You are probably very accomplished
and, employing clear logic, initiate projects and achieve results. You
enjoy language and you are warm and expansive.

You have a fine, refined mind which can pierce the veils and look
underneath the surface. The individual instruments, especially the instruments in the background, have great clarity for you, and this
demonstrates the clarity of your thinking. You can take a small aspect,
bring it in, and weigh it into the equation and make sense of the
whole.

There is a soft sensitivity, almost magical, which you illustrate.
There is something of an illustrator in you. The ability to illustrate a
point of view.

You are aware of reincarnation and karma. Your energy field
seems to feel this. You are a highly intelligent individual, very interested in what's going on in life and uncovering the hidden meanings.
You feel very moved by this music and may want to uncover the mys-

teries of life. The sound of the harmonica also touches you (and probably the word "harmony" would be significant for you too). There is a sense of a longing in the harmonica; it captures what you are trying to achieve down here. The bass guitar at the back of the music is also lovely for you.

Your energy field is showing a split. One side is open to discovering the hidden meaning to life. This emanates from your intellectual capacities. Your intellect is strong. However, your intellect has not succeeded in discovering the experience of this hidden meaning. If you are after this experience, I suggest meditation. Of course, there are many other avenues as well.

Absolutely beautiful.

Client Feedback

"First let me thank you for taking the time to analyze my choice of song, I found it to be clear, precise and frankly quite accurate. I especially liked and respect your spiritual approach. May I ask you about your obvious gifts you have in the field? I am a palmist and tarot student, and have worked in these mainstream fields over many years. I found your take to be very accurate, rather penetrating and sympathetic. How could I not agree with your kind comments! I am very interested in all matters metaphysical and spiritual.

Thanks again,"

William

CHAPTER FIFTEEN

"Diamondize" performed by Wide Eyes

If this is your favorite song, then you are probably special in these ways:

- Unpredictable
- Creative
- At home with abstract qualities of thought
- Intellectual
- Intense
- Imaginative
- Express inspiration
- Express originality
- Open to possibilities and alternative viewpoints
- Adventurous
- An expression of speed and an expression of light
- Possess hidden depths in your personality

Client: Curtis

It has been a pleasure to intuit this Song Read for you. I had not heard this music before. What an exciting choice of music!

I interpret your deeper connection to the song in this way:

You display the unexpected, the frantic and the creative. Music is very open to interpretation, and you are also open to different interpretations. You enjoy and are at home with abstract qualities of thought, and with creativity. You want to express intellect, intensity, focus, thought, imagination and inspiration. This is an exciting choice of music for you. There is a sense of speed, of speed of light. You are very open to possibilities.

You sometimes behave in an unexpected way. The planet Uranus comes to mind. (The planet Uranus rules originality, inventions, future events, rebellion and new world order.) Perhaps you are comfortable with abrupt changes. You are open to different viewpoints, adventure, surprises, and are able to cope with these well. The music is clear, not clouded. It has an expectant clear quality to it. I sense a frantic pace; planet Uranus is jumping in and causing turmoil. The other planet expressed here is Mercury (the planet of thought, intellect and communication). I also perceive a sprinkling of planet Jupiter, the planet of higher learning, philosophy and good luck. Jupiter adds beneficence, a beneficence of energy to this music and to you.

There is a sense of joy, a sense of climbing up, an expression of speed and an expression of light. You like the abstract. In many ways this music expresses energy forms, too. The music makes me think of a clear prism with multicolored lights entering it and refracting off it in different directions. The music shows you a huge range of possibilities and it reminds you to keep open to alternate viewpoints.

The crescendo is very enjoyable and we are taken along on the journey toward the climax, which also symbolizes our "highs" in life. I can imagine you playing along to this music, jumping around to this sound as it frees you to a certain extent. The music connects you to a sense of freedom within you. The music also connects you to a sense of hope, and you enjoy these connections to the deeper aspects. This music helps you soar and experience the heights and is perfect for you as an artist and abstract expressionist. I am smiling while I am intuiting this read and I sense that you smile when you listen to this music.

Quite a lot of this sound appears to be expressing the light, the speed of light, the reflection and the refraction of light and it is expressing through your temple chakras, which have access to higher energy interpretations. The music plays in your head and intellectual faculties.

The journey of the music is very beneficial to you and it shows us that we all want to arrive at the end destination, but the journey and the process and the twists and turns of the process are really enlivening.

With multiple listens to this music, the nuances are more pronounced, the subtleties, which you would be aware of, become far more evident. The complexity of the music becomes far more evident. There is a sense of hidden depths and the sense of more to be discovered. All these aspects of the music are within you and expressions of you.

I love the build-up and the crescendo at the end. It must give you a great "high!"

CHAPTER SIXTEEN

"Downpressor Man" performed by Sinead O'Connor

If this is your favorite song, then you are probably special in these ways:

- Gentle
- Calm
- Receptive
- Creative
- Emotive
- Intuitive and open to subtleties
- Have a vision which is very encompassing
- Observant
- Aware of the deeper and profound meanings in life
- Complex
- Quirky
- Insightful

Client: Benjamin

I have so enjoyed intuiting this Song Read for you. I had not heard this music before.

I interpret your deeper connection to the song in this way:

There is gentleness in you. This song connects you, and is like a stream up through your body and to The Divine. It is akin to a ribbon. You are gentle and calm and receptive.

You probably prefer to process through your right brain. You are creative, emotive and intuitive. You are open to subtleties. You like subtleties. You pick up the subtleties in most situations. You are highly intuitive as well. You have a nice clear energy field. You appear to be very gentle and you express the sound of a tinkle, a light, clear ringing sound, similar to a chime. You perhaps do not like the logical side and approaching life from logic, but I sense that you are quite talented at math.

You have far sight—your vision is very encompassing. You have what looks like a lighthouse in your ajna chakra. You are highly observant and you take in more than most people. Your sense of observation is acute. You don't necessarily like what you see and your judgment may mar your observations to some degree.

You possess a nice sound when you laugh and smile. You possess feminine, receptive, yin energy. There appears to be a secret knowing in you. You can be a touch cynical. You tend to look for the deeper, profound meaning in life.

Your heart is open. You are a gentle soul. Are you searching for something? You like the swearing at the end of the song and it makes you laugh. There is freshness to you. You can be a bit coy. You are complex, soft, gentle and quirky, and can easily see the hidden dimensions of life. I think of the symbol; "the court jester." It is as if you have a secret meaning to share with people. You probably appreciate satire. I see the tinkling energy patterns; I hear the tinkling sounds in you. You are happy. I also sense "The Joker" (as in Batman) and the symbolic archetype "the jester" in you. You are an amusing person with the ability to mask your capability for insight and advice with satire and jest. This is the image I have of you. You are a bit mischievous, devilish.

You understand the lyrics well. You can present as cryptic. You are a talented observer and occasionally cynical. I sense that you prefer observing to participating.

"Perception" is a word that comes to mind for you.

CHAPTER SEVENTEEN

"Dreamer Deceiver" performed by Judas Priest

If this is your favorite song, then you are probably special in these ways:

- Sensitive
- Reflective and pensive
- Curious and questioning
- Artistic and poetic
- A profound personality
- Gentle
- Have a yearning desire for…
- An intimate and giving soul
- Open to emotions
- Think deeply
- Optimistic
- Complex
- Spiritual
- A creative intellectual

Client: Liam

It has been a pleasure to intuit this Song Read for you. I had not heard this music before. This interpretation is particularly abstract.

I interpret your deeper connection to the song in this way:

You are sensitive, reflective, questioning and at times can be sad. You have an artistic personality. You are profound and artistic and gentle. I feel the lyrics are important to you. A deeper meaning is held within the lyrics for you.

There is a longing in you too. This sound lifts you up to the heavens. It connects you to Source. You appear to be lifted up as if through your antakarana. (The Hindu Sanskrit word antakarana refers to the central column of energy, running through the body connecting us to The Divine and to The Earth. It is the bridge between our higher and lower consciousness.) This song energetically goes to the back of your head and this area is wide open to receive. It is as if your angel wings are right up here at the back of your head.

There is some energy congestion over your left ajna and left eye which seems to indicate some blockages with creative vision. There appears to be some wounds to the left eye. Actually it may be the other way around too, with your left eye almost acting as your spiritual eye for you.

You are an intimate soul and you give of yourself quite beautifully. You are pensive, open to your emotions and think very deeply. You resonate with the sound of the electric guitar and the drum beating in the background. You really resonate with this combination. There seems to be some truth for you here in these lyrics. There is a journey, an epic element here for you. And there is love here for you too. Perhaps you do not find it easy to express the depth of your love in the way you would like to. It is almost as if the crying vocal is also finding it hard to express what you are trying to express.

Now we are entering a different tempo. Just like the journey of life. We are getting prepared for the next stage of life. You are optimistic and ready to rock and roll. You are a complex character. There is a bit of a panic, a bit of a hurry up, hurry up. You want to arrive but perhaps sometimes you are not noticing the journey in your haste. You are able to laugh and enjoy yourself. The faster aspects of the music seem to suggest the physical world for you. You are able to see the difference between this physical world and the spiritual world. And you exist in both worlds and probably spend most of your time in the physical world, like most of us do. But the music slows down at the end of the song and it raises you right up to the spiritual world again and it is an immediate connection for you.

There is an interesting aspect about happiness. We are searching for it and we are not sure where to go to find it. Happiness is inside of us. Paramahansa Yogananda, an Indian yogi and Guru, teaches, "Although happiness depends to some extent upon external conditions, it depends chiefly upon conditions of the inner mind."

Your hands are in the upward and outward position, and up we go. When you rise up to The Divine, the energy on your left shoulder seems to hurt a bit. It is a little bit disjointed when you rise up. Perhaps you suffer from a lack of trust. You are very curious to find out about the spiritual realm, which impresses you and you desire it. But your left shoulder is pulling you down to Earth. You seem to be feeling a lack of sufficient trust. You are an aware soul and you feel comfortable, maybe not understanding, that your aura and energy field is clear and so you feel comfort. You like this sense of comfort and clarity.

These are fabulous lyrics for you. The artist and poet within you love these lyrics. Sound moves you and if you listen very carefully, in the silence you can hear the sound "Om." You are deep, poetic, spiritual and the lyrics help to express the depth of you, the depth of your emotion and the depth of your intellect. You are a creative intellectual. These are great wonderful spiritual lyrics. I'm sure you pay attention to the lyrics and they can help you. I wonder if you want freedom, and if you are looking for freedom in other worlds and realms.

CHAPTER EIGHTEEN

"Feel the Love" performed by Rudimental

If this is your favorite song, then you are probably special in these ways:

- A loving Spirit
- Joyful
- Upbeat and happy
- Full of feelings and love
- Express love easily
- Connected to the universal element of love
- Share and give love
- Love your fellow human beings
- Accepting of others
- Express innocence
- Have clarity and profundity of understanding
- Open to intuition
- Receptive
- Balanced

Client: Ava

It has been a pleasure to intuit this Song Read for you. I had not heard this music before.

I interpret your deeper connection to the song in this way:

This song expands your energy field. Your aura is pushing out-wards and you are very connected to Source and The Divine pours energy down on you. The crescendo in the music enters straight into your heart chakra.

The music is quite techno and you seem to be very at home with this beat. There is a little bit of energetic static down on your right side. Your logic almost asks you, "Why do you like this song?" You can query why you like this song a lot, but it is The Joy in you which likes this song. And now the energetic static goes away. Your logic doesn't need to be your logic. Why do you like this song? You just do!

You're very upbeat. This music lifts you easily and the saxophone and trumpet make you feel happy, happy. You seem to be directly communicating with Source. It is as if choir boys are singing to you. This song, for you, expresses love. The feeling goes through your arms, which are connected to your heart chakra. You are full of feel-ing. You are full of love. You and the energy within you become very big and expansive listening to this song.

There doesn't seem to be anything else to add! You express your own love easily. The lyrics are very self-explanatory. This song con-nects you to love, to the universal element of love, to the sharing element of love, to your love of your fellow human beings and your acceptance of all of us in the human race.

You may probably want to dance with your friends to this song. You can express innocence, and innocence can give you clarity and profundity of understanding.

If music and a song can expand an energy field to this level, it has to be good for you!

I'm a convert. I like this song too now!

P.S.

A few words to add: a great wide smile, sharing, joy, open to intuition, receptive, giving and balance.

Client Feedback

"Awen,

Thank you so much for this. I just love the explanation. It rings very true for me. Much love,"

Ava

CHAPTER NINETEEN

"Fix You" performed by Coldplay

If this is your favorite song, then you are probably special in these ways:

- Dramatic
- Ethereal
- Delicate
- Refined
- Innately courageous and confident
- Developing self-worth and self-love
- Developing authenticity
- Sensitive
- Empathetic
- Passionate
- Behave consciously (as in awareness of what you are doing)
- Open to magic

Client: Josh

It has been a pleasure to intuit this Song Read for you. I had not heard this music before.

I interpret your deeper connection to the song in this way:

This singer has a certain amount of drama about him, and this sense of drama is also in you. The singer's voice at times has an ethereal quality and he reaches other realms. This music connects you to Source. You are also delicate and refined.

It appears that you have had quite a bit of hardship and sadness. Perhaps this song is autobiographical for you? Songs are open to interpretation and I offer but one interpretation here. One of the challenges for humankind today is the need for many of us to develop our feelings of self-worth and self-love. This song may also present the ultimate solution to this challenge. And so this song may have a deeper spiritual meaning and you are connecting with this deeper spiritual meaning.

It seems that you are being asked to grow your innate characteristics of courage, confidence, self-worth, self-love and authenticity and to bring your real "you" into the world. This appears to be a very common challenge for mankind at the moment. You are not alone here. Be patient. Few of us realize that we do not need to go around trying to change others. At the same time, we need to accept that we really don't need to be changed either. There is some sense of defiance here for you. You are quite defiant and rebellious and understand that it is wrong for you to be mistreated. And conversely you probably also understand it is wrong for you to mistreat others. You are also highly sensitive, a quality which you have earned from past pain. This sensitivity allows you to connect with others and to express empathy. You are learning how to be compassionate with yourself and with others.

There is passion here and within you. The second half of the song is quite uplifting, and it is acting consciously (as in awareness of what it is doing). It is helpful allowing the emotion to be expressed, because the emotion would only become stuck and affect us negatively. It is helpful to stand in the power of who we are. And perhaps standing in the power of who we really are is home. Your higher self is smiling in happiness here. This message is possibly relevant for many of us.

Another lesson is to acknowledge the pain which has been received, to allow that emotion to come out, and to forgive. It is possible that some of this story may have happened to you in your childhood, and you have probably, like many of us, been taught not to cry. But that's really not healthy for any of us. It is not healthy or natural to not cry.

There is magic within you, expressed by the piano sound. The piano in the middle of the song is like birds flying. And this is really what is around the corner for you.

CHAPTER TWENTY

"Grace" performed by Jeff Buckley

If this is your favorite song, then you are probably special in these ways:

- Open to new experiences
- Intellectual
- Creative
- Charming
- Complex
- Talented with both rationalism & logic and intuition & creativity
- Sensitive to energy impressions
- Appreciate the arts and the creative process
- Thrive being around creative people
- A naturally-talented person in many areas
- Feel deeply
- Possess street credibility

Client: Gabriel

It has been a pleasure to intuit this Song Read for you.

I interpret your deeper connection to the song in this way:

You are the wanderer and the traveler. You enjoy life. You are open to new experiences, new contacts, and new "highs." You are an intellectual person, a thinker. You possess connection to spirit. You possess openness and you are a creative person with some charm. The sound of the riffs of the guitar holds joy for you. And I see you and sense you most easily through these guitar riffs. You are quite a complex character.

You can actually live very well in both your right brain and your left brain. But this can also create confusion for you. Many people tend to be dominant in either the logical left or the creative right, and approach life in a very one-sided way. You tend to be open to both. You feel the pull of both ways and this can make it quite difficult to walk a central path of ease, being aware of both the necessity for rationalism and logic and also the necessity for intuition and creativity.

You pick up on and sense a lot of the vibes and energy impressions from the people around you. Meditation would probably be of benefit to you, providing a sense of internal peace and freedom.

I sense a very masculine person. I feel that you are creative and that is why you are attracted to this singer and this song. There is a genuine appreciation of the arts and you enjoy and thrive being around creative people. You easily appreciate the creative process and genius behind art, music and drama. There is some sense of chaos in the song, and there seems to be very much that sense of chaos with you, but it is probably the split personality within you. You have within you the ability to successfully bring your skills and talents to many areas of life. Whatever path you take, your natural talents will help you. You are a naturally talented person in many areas.

There are some obstacles and fuzziness in communication, maybe some blockages in talking clearly. At times there seems to be some energy blockage between your head and your heart. The signals between your head and heart are not always in harmony. One tends to overtake the other, and this can create a few difficulties for you at times.

Fire has the element of healing and transformation. Maybe you are aware of some underlying forces going on in life. There is a subtle awareness here for you and you can't ignore these forces as they keep presenting themselves to you.

You don't seem to like time and I think the reason for this is because in the spirit world there is no time. Energy works through time, space and dimensions. Linear time doesn't exist. Maybe you happen to remember this fact.

There is melancholy within you. You feel deeply. You may also have had some pain and so you can connect to this song. The words and pain have gone deep and they shape you. When you were in pain, it didn't appear that you had a support system in place to help you, and so you were very much left to deal with this on your own. This song allows you to open up to those emotions a little. Often we pretend that those dark, hurtful emotions are not happening. We swallow them, sit on them, and pretend that we don't hurt. We want to protect ourselves, protect our ego, which is not necessarily a helpful way to be, or to process the pain, but it is what many of us do.

There is also the sense of an image with this song. The desire to say something about your image, which you choose to project outwards. An image of "cred" (as in street credibility) which helps to identify you.

"Ethereal" is a word you may like.

Client Feedback

"Hi Awen

Well you were pretty much dead on. The masculine part is right, I'm pretty much the alpha male, though highly sensitive as well.

What you said about left brain right brain is me as well. I very much use both, and have some difficulty balancing it off. Same with head and heart, though they may be the same things really.

Also, you are correct in saying I do well with whatever I turn my mind to. I'm very good at anything I apply myself to. I have done a lot of things and am quite accomplished with them. I can paint, play music, I can design and build a house on my own, and I can program computers. I can sail.

And you're really dead on when you say I don't like time, no I don't, and can't bend it and slow it and speed it up at will. I don't like the restriction or the illusion of it.

Anyway, I thought that was a pretty good reading altogether and I have had a lot of readings in my time. I'm quite 'psychic' myself. I'm pretty surprised you can get all that from a song. Good going. Thank you for it and all the best! I wonder what you would make of my own songs?"

Gabriel

CHAPTER TWENTY-ONE

"Home Sweet Home" performed by Motley Crue

If this is your favorite song, then you are probably special in these ways:

- Possess a great sense of humor
- Fun
- Quirky and eccentric
- Very much an individual
- Enjoy being with a group of friends
- A great friend
- Appreciate traditional values
- Optimist
- Passionate
- Big-hearted
- Joyful
- A dreamer

Client: Adrian

I have so enjoyed intuiting this Song Read for you. I was not familiar with this song.

I interpret your deeper connection to the song in this way:

You possess a great sense of humor. You are great fun and you enjoy laughing. You are quirky and groovy and are very much an individual. You enjoy being with a group of friends, sharing common interests and goals. You are a great friend to have. Traditional values are important to you. You are also an optimist.

This music enables you to express your feelings and emotions, which at other times you may find more difficult to do. There are probably times when you find it far more difficult to express your point of view. There is deep passion in you and you experience the full array of emotions, from pain and hurt to pleasure, love and joy. This song seems to make you feel "All is well in my world."

Your energy field magnifies considerably when this music is with you. It pulls you up and you become at home with your feelings and emotions, which flow easily through you when you are with this song. You possess a big heart. You smile a lot and there is a sense great joy here for you.

The dreamer in you is alive and well and nourished. This song also helps you to express a wilder aspect of yourself. You seem to feel an affinity with the eccentricities of the band members.

The guitar sounds are very rousing for you. You love this song. You are very connected to The Divine through this music. You connect easily to Source. I sense The Divine pouring heaps of energy down on you. It showers down upon you with divine love and connection. With this music you express absolute joy. There is extreme joy here for you. And this music opens you to feel freedom. This music seems to totally free you; your heart chakra is huge, you sense freedom.

There are some energetic tears of sadness behind your eyes in the gentler music riffs at the end of the song, as you very easily and quickly return to the real world from your dreams and your imagination, but you have a longing for another realm. This music gives you release and you feel that you can be yourself and express the deeper passions that are within you. You like the connection to passion and emotional feeling which this song provides for you. You are then able to more easily express these elements of yourself.

CHAPTER TWENTY-TWO

"How We Operate" performed by Gomez

If this is your favorite song, then you are probably special in these ways:

- Intellectual
- Safe
- Clever
- Protective
- Interested in understanding…
- Inquisitive
- On a quest to find meaning
- Potential for emotional clarity
- Potential for easy understanding
- Potential to work through your heart

Client: Charlotte

It has been a pleasure to intuit this Song Read for you. I had not heard this music before.

I interpret your deeper connection to the song in this way:

You like the sound of the string instruments. When the tempo in the music picks up speed, you connect to Source.

Your intellect appears to push outward. You like this song intellectually. You enjoy the mix of the sound and the singer's voice. You work well with your intellect.

It seems that you keep yourself safe in your own energy field, without offering information to me. I am asking you what you would like to tell me. I sense that you are a clever individual. You seem to be protecting yourself.

There appears to be some disparity between the sounds and the voice. This indicates you tend to make issues more complicated than they need to be.

Also you are looking to understand, to get to the bottom of things. You are inquisitive. You are on a quest to find meaning.

When we leave the head, the mind space, and go into the louder, more rousing, emotional music, you drop your reliance on the mind and you seem to have more emotional clarity. Your life is much happier when you process through the head, but you appear to see more clearly when you process through your emotions. It just is.

I sense that maybe you have a desire to be right. You seem to be getting a bit caught up in your own cleverness.

I perceive that you enjoy the sentiment of the lyrics. I think you are possibly looking for a deeper meaning in some issues in relationships. I sense you are endeavoring to get to the bottom of things. You also seem to be working in your head. If you choose to work through your heart, and to allow yourself to feel the power in some of these adjectives within the lyrics, you will actually have an easy understanding. The message is for you to choose to come out of your head and experiment processing through your heart. You will be able to see and you will be able to understand more easily. You have a wonderful capacity to work through your heart, you are just choosing to process through your head.

These lyrics have meaning for you. They are asking you to consider change and to accept that there could be another way. I sense that you are aware of this. The lyrics are not talking to somebody else, they are talking to you, so that you can become more balanced and internally have more peace and harmony.

CHAPTER TWENTY-THREE

"I Am The Walrus" performed by The Beatles

If this is your favorite song, then you are probably special in these ways:

- Unique and unusual
- Dramatic
- Creative
- Open to the new
- Enjoy the abstract and the obscure
- Desire to shock
- Fun
- Aware of the masks we wear in society
- Aware of the paradoxes in society
- Have a great sense of humor
- Desire a spiritual element to life
- Intellectual
- Insightful
- Ahead of your time

Client: Lachlan

It has been a pleasure to intuit this Song Read for you.

I interpret your deeper connection to the song in this way:

You are a unique, dramatic and unusual individual. There are unusual sounds here. You are creative and open to the new. You enjoy the abstract and the obscure. At times you suffer from deep cynicism. There is light and dark displayed here. There is also a hint of confusion. There is both separateness but at the same time connection to Spirit, as I sense an open crown chakra. These alternatives of separation and connection to Spirit exist for you. The music can appear confrontational and has a desire to shock. The lyrics raise us out of our group malaise and there is a good deal of fun here too. These are all qualities which you possess.

Maybe you have previously suffered from some emotional hurt and so you choose to look at life a tad cynically. I sense this song is nudging you to find peace in your heart. Perhaps it is because this song is expressed through your head that we need to revert to the opening lines, which are about spirit. There is a hint of a slightly clouded vision. There is some chaos in the ajna chakra, a hint of chaos with your expanded vision and big picture view of life.

You enjoy interpreting the lyrics. You understand the masks we wear in society and how these are often not helpful and how we can deceive ourselves. You are very aware of the paradoxes in society and you find humor in this awareness. You have a great sense of humor and you are making me laugh! You are aware of the joke of what people are doing; for are we not often unaware of what we are doing?

You desire a spiritual element to life and you are possibly aware that we are also what we are looking at. Other people are a mirror to us. We are all one. You wish for life to be simple, for life to be honest and open.

This is an intellectual song with insightful lyrics and this insight is within you too. In many ways you are ahead of your time with your insight. You are probably geared to the future. The insight in the music is hidden within the story of the lyrics. This also often happened with mystical teachings—the teaching was hidden in stories for the spiritual seeker to uncover. This music expresses your intellectual capacities, rather than your emotions. I sense a detached feeling, that you are more an observer of life than a participant.

You are aware that, as humans, we put up little devices to obscure the spiritual truth. We all do this.

Client Feedback

"Hi

Thank you for your interpretation of my favorite song. A lot does apply to me. I'm interested in what other people's favorite songs are. I like "I'm the walrus," it is an old song but hasn't dated. I don't know why this is, when other songs are forgotten after a short time. Why does a song have longevity when others don't?"

Lachlan

CHAPTER TWENTY-FOUR

"I Don't Wanna Miss a Thing" performed by Aerosmith

If this is your favorite song, then you are probably special in these ways:

- Have a beautiful big heart
- Express love and receive love
- Grateful
- Appreciative
- Compassionate
- Joyful
- Content
- Have a soft sense of humor
- Dramatic
- Comfortable expressing yourself
- Happy to be in a group
- Access the big-picture vision of life
- Have integrity
- Genuine

Client: Rachael

It has been a pleasure to intuit this Song Read for you.

I interpret your deeper connection to the song in this way:

Already we are moving into the great ethereal realm. There is the sense of an epic about to unfold. You are smiling broadly and you have a beautiful big heart and you possess the qualities of the heart. You express love and receive love very easily. You show gratitude and appreciation and compassion. I am actually laughing while interpreting this song. You are making me laugh. This music very much connects you to Source. This is a big number, a big song.

You have your arms held upwards and outwards and you are full of emotion with this song. This connects you very easily. From time to time you express tears of joy. You also express great contentment, and you seem to have the protection of an angel at your back.

You must have a soft sense of humor, perhaps cheeky, silly and silky humor, because I am laughing so much! There is an element of drama in you. You are comfortable expressing yourself. You are happy to be in a group.

You easily access the big-picture vision of life. You are an individual who walks their talk. As in, you have integrity.

You are very connected to Source from your heart chakra up to your crown chakra. You demonstrate an abundance of love and people watch you doing this. In this way you are a very good teacher. You are genuine and others pick this up in you. And you are still making me laugh so much!

This song sits beautifully in your energy field and it expands your energy field.

There is the sense of an orchestra in the musical sound, as if the orchestra is going to help to express the power and fullness of this love. You love this song. It seems to express you very well. You easily understand the lyrics. You fully understand the importance of love down here, and my only addition is that this could be interpreted to mean both physical love and spiritual love.

This song and the music and the lyrics and the orchestra well up inside you, and you find it exceedingly easy to express the energy of this song because the energy of this song is within you too.

Client Feedback

"I love this! You did such a great job. Thank you :) I have already recommended you to my aunt and a friend, just seconds after reading it. That is just amazing. I love it."

Rachael

CHAPTER TWENTY-FIVE

"I Guess the Lord Must Be in New York City" performed by Harry Nilsson

If this is your favorite song, then you are probably special in these ways:

- Humorous
- Have lightness in your thoughts
- Possess an easy smile
- Possess an easy, effortless nature
- Innocent
- Comfortable in yourself
- Popular
- In the "now"
- A giving spirit
- Find it easy to let go
- Accepting
- Optimistic
- Sincere
- Expectant of good things to come

Client: Kayde

It has been a pleasure to intuit this Song Read for you.

I interpret your deeper connection to the song in this way:

You are making me laugh so much! This song connects you beautifully. You are very clear and light and your thoughts are very light. There is an ease to you and to your personality. You possess an easy smile, an easy nature, innocence, and you are comfortable and popular. You have innocence in your energy field. It is as if the little boy in you in some way never grew up, which is a nice free quality to have. So you treat the day with freshness and you find it very easy to be in the "now."

You find it easy to give and easy to let go and release yourself from minor challenges. You don't over-think or over-complicate matters, and you are also accepting rather than judgmental. You are very optimistic, light and airy. You have an easy freedom within your energy field. This song has a welcoming easy freedom and comfort. Both nouns seem to express you really well. That guitar riff really hooks you in. The lyrics are obvious for you.

I sense the deeper meaning is that this music connects you to an ease and grace where you feel at home and comfortable. There is innocence, sincerity, an easy expectancy of good things to come and an easy acceptance here.

CHAPTER TWENTY-SIX

"Impossible" performed by Something for Kate

If this is your favorite song, then you are probably special in these ways:

- Sensitive
- Open to other realms
- Possess softness and deepness
- Feel deeply and are receptive to emotions
- Have profound thoughts
- Possess street credibility
- Respectful
- Connect intimately one to one
- Talented at the art of listening
- Passionate
- Understand the abstract
- Willing to change and progress
- Empathetic
- Compassionate

Client: Vincent

It has been an absolute pleasure to intuit this Song Read for you. I had not heard this music before. What a beautiful song!

I interpret your deeper connection to the song in this way:

A vision comes to mind: The wanderer, wandering through fields and the desert. Alone, but not lonely. You have sensitivity and openness to other realms; you have a connection to Source and Spirit. When you let in The Divine and open up your crown chakra, a great deal of uplifting bliss comes in. Maybe you are not aware when you are doing this. You possess softness and deepness.

You feel very deeply. You have possibly suffered some pain, and through this you connect to others. You possess depth, profundity of emotion and thought. This gives you a lot of credibility and respect. There is also a lot of silence, especially in group settings. You connect intimately one-to-one. You are talented at the art of listening.

You are open to other worlds. But maybe you are not around people who are, and perhaps you feel the need to be quiet and silent about this area of your understanding. This is deeply personal for you, and you may feel safer if you have your defenses up, because we can be mocked when we talk spiritual language.

It appears the message is that you have within you the power to make anything happen. It may be helpful for you to have someone who can connect with this side of you.

Aspects of deep passion are very apparent. The music is very passionate and plunges the depths. There is deep feeling and deep passion. You must be a very passionate person. You may not necessarily be vocal in this passion, but within, you are passionate. You feel passionately and deeply. This is such a beautiful quality in you. You can help other people see the underlying meanings in life events. There is a redemptive quality as a consequence of all this passion.

You have an understanding of the abstract. The abstractness of existence and of life.

Your angel is with you, and she is a female angel!

Your connection to these lyrics suggests you remember other lives, a life before this incarnation. You yearn to learn more about your soul, about other realms. It would be nice for you to have someone to share this aspect of yourself with. And you will learn from this that everybody is connected in this same way. Your energy can at times be ethereal, it can ebb and flow and it can be cleansing. There is the ability to change and progress within you.

You are receptive to your emotions. You have great empathy and compassion for people who suffer and you enjoy lending a helping hand.

A beautiful song for you.

CHAPTER TWENTY-SEVEN

"In My Darkest Hour" performed by Megadeth

If this is your favorite song, then you are probably special in these ways:

- Have a yearning desire for…
- Have a sense of destiny
- Potential to be a soothing influence on others
- Potential to flow with life's ups and downs
- Poetic
- Passionate
- Protective
- Understand the dichotomy of anger and fear, pain and love

Client: Justin

It has been a pleasure to intuit this Song Read for you. I had not heard this music before.

I interpret your deeper connection to the song in this way:

The music at the beginning sits well with you. There is a longing in both you and in the music at the commencement of the song. However, the heavier tones seem to work as an obstacle, a kind of oppression, for you, a sense of destiny and a sense of anger. You appear to have some difficulty expressing and working with your emotions. You probably have some communication issues, due perhaps, to a reluctance to show who you really are.

I am receiving the image of a soft light blue color for you, which is a cool, soothing color. This color would probably be of help to you.

This song and the accompanying music connect your crown chakra to Source, but it fuzzes up other chakras in you. There may be issues around the sinus, and you may suffer from headaches at the back of your head.

As the tempo of the music increases pace, it seems to indicate that you're racing ahead and not really paying attention to the signposts, to the little details which can be of help to you. You seem to be missing them.

The soft guitar sound at the beginning of the track is more allowing and flowing for you and you become less resistant to outside stimuli.

The lyrics are strung together very poetically, and they illustrate the theme very well. You like the lyrics. Energetically this sound cuts through your cheekbones. The energy seems to run through your cheeks which are on the same horizontal axis as the ears. Perhaps there are blockages between your communication and higher vision. I sense that you maybe do not believe this song. A belief isn't truth, it is a choice. You can at times have some difficulty expressing the higher vision.

There is passion within you. There are perhaps issues which symbolize rejection, or lack of security. You seem to hold quite a lot of anger. Perhaps you don't really believe these lyrics, but they help you express pain, anger and betrayal. This song seems to be presenting you with your issues. You may not be aware of this. I think that this is a helpful song for you. It is illustrating some areas which may be helpful for you to look at and consider.

Now the music seems to be wrapping around you like a shield. A shield of armor to protect you from pain. At the end of the song we revert back into some soft tones. You understand the dichotomy of anger and fear, pain and love.

CHAPTER TWENTY-EIGHT

"It's My Life" performed by Bon Jovi

If this is your favorite song, then you are probably special in these ways:

- Have an abundant source of energy
- Enjoy being with friends
- Fun
- Refreshing
- Upbeat
- Have a warm personality
- Balanced between head and heart
- Express intellect and emotions easily
- Appreciate unity consciousness
- Assertive and independent
- Confident and stand up for yourself
- Protective

Client: Emma

It has been a pleasure to intuit this Song Read for you.

I interpret the hidden messages in your favorite song in this way:

You enjoy this sound and you can give yourself over to this sound quite easily. You enjoy singing along to these lyrics as well. You have an abundant source of energy. This music connects you to Source.

You enjoy being with your friends and you like having a good time. There is a lot of fun in you and you enjoy experiencing fun. You are refreshing, upbeat and have a warm personality. You are balanced between your head and your heart and express your intellect and emotions easily.

You appreciate the "anthem" quality to the lyrics. You would possibly derive pleasure from singing along to these lyrics with a group of like-minded souls. You like the sense of "unity consciousness," which is the sense that "all is one."

You are fond of the lyrics and identify with them. You like feeling alive and living life in your own way and on your own terms. You thoroughly agree with the sentiment of the lyrics. You are assertive, independent and confident. You stand up for yourself and you protect your friends.

I sense this song in your head. This indicates that you intellectually like this song, rather than have a heart-based love of this song. However, it seems that your rational brain doesn't fully believe the viability of the sentiment of the lyrics. I perceive that you would love to live with the self-responsibility these lyrics talk about, but perhaps you don't do this all of the time. Many of us are tied to old habits and conditions, so it is very difficult to live life, all the time, the way we want to. Our behavior is often determined by unconscious drives and needs. To actually do what these lyrics say is harder than it may at first appear. I think you appreciate this. It doesn't happen easily. We have to take risks, take full responsibility for our lives and understand that there are consequences to our actions. It seems that these lyrics are a great goal for you to pursue. These lyrics will help to give you guidance and direction. Maybe think about these lyrics when considering choices in your life and on your journey.

So it appears that the hidden message for you within the lyrics is that they offer guidance for the big picture of your life. When you need to make important decisions or choose between different paths, consider this

CHAPTER TWENTY-NINE

"Kashmir" performed by Led Zeppelin

If this is your favorite song, then you are probably special in these ways

- Dramatic
- Believe in fate and destiny
- Open to spirituality
- Big-hearted
- Steady and sure
- Intuitive and open to dreams
- Reserved
- Tolerant and patient
- Dependable and responsible
- Desire spontaneity
- A formidable opponent
- Creative
- Sexy
- Far-sighted and think deeply

Client: Joshua
It has been a pleasure to intuit this Song Read for you. I had not heard this music before.

I interpret your deeper connection to the song in this way:

There is drama within you. You have an understanding of the inevitable destiny of life. You have an easy connection to Source. You are open to spirituality and the invisible. You possess a wide heart and surety. You are open to intuition and other realms. You are open to dreams and possibly receive information and signs in dreams.

Sometimes you can over-think matters and at times you may give too much credence to your thinking, rational brain. You enjoy a good strong laugh. You appear to be more reserved in personality than expressive. But there is still a sense of drama about you. You are tolerant and patient. You seem to believe in fate and destiny. This song connects you very easily to Source, right up through your spine, behind the ajna chakra right up to The Divine. You are very connected with this energy. You also have a very steady energy field. You are a dependable and responsible individual. But you don't happen to appreciate these qualities much and you perhaps don't like it when these qualities run your life. You have some internal frustration if you are not in a position where you can express your deeper feelings.

You enjoy these lyrics. They have meaning for you. You have a sense of the various stages of life we go through. You accept this. However, you secretly crave the unexpected, and desire to have more spontaneity in your life.

You can be obstinate at times. You are so steady and sure. You would be a formidable opponent. In a challenge you would probably win, because you have the foresight to work through the various scenarios and outcomes before they happen. You are ahead of other people in this way. You can figure out what others are going to do before they do it. But this preoccupation also takes up energy from yourself, where it may be more helpfully spent.

You appear to have a very masculine personality. There is a quality of a journey, a quality of an epic in this music for you. You enjoy the voice of the lead singer. I sense the voice quality helps you to open up to your own emotional, sexy side. You are a creative individual and you enjoy the complexity, the depth and the far reach of these lyrics. This song also helps you express your inner passions. This song expands you in many ways. These are great poetic lyrics. You understand the lyrics and gain meaning from them.

You very much appreciate the genius, creativity, far-sightedness, depth of understanding and depth of openness in this song. These qualities are also present within you.

CHAPTER THIRTY

"Learn To Fly" performed by Shannon Noll

If this is your favorite song, then you are probably special in these ways:

- Romantic
- Happy
- A peaceful spirit
- Have a clear and open personality
- Sincere
- Open-hearted
- Communicate clearly
- Wish well for everybody
- Loving
- Joyous
- Truthful
- Confident and courageous

Client: Ian

It has been a pleasure to intuit this Song Read for you. I had not heard this music before.

I interpret your deeper connection to the song in this way:

You are a romantic, happy and peaceful soul. You have a clear and open personality. This song connects you to Source, and the chorus raises you and fills you with love. I can sense you singing along to this song. You are peace-loving, romantic and sincere. You are a sincere soul with an open heart. You desire and enjoy connecting with others. You communicate quite easily and clearly.

You hope for good things and good events in the world, and you hope for good things and good times for yourself. You tend to wish well for everybody, which is a beautiful quality to possess.

I can see you with your arms open. There is a lot of love in you. You want to embrace life and embrace people.

You may at times present as a little bit over-emotional and this can be difficult for others, who jump to defense. Perhaps on occasion you may be a little bit free with your emotions. It may be helpful to introduce a boundary to help with the level of emotion you express.

You are a beautiful and joyous soul and you have come down to this world to share joy and love. This song easily connects you with The Divine. This song seems to be quite perfect for you.

The lyrics of this song contain helpful advice for you. At times of struggle, it shows you where to go and how to behave. I think you naturally do this. You do not seem to be upset by the difficulties and challenges of life, like many of us are. It seems that you cope well.

Flying is probably one of your dreams, because if you could fly or bi-locate, (appear in two places at the same time) you could be with everybody immediately, connect with more people, sharing your love and joy. You are a truthful person. Remember that fear is the absence of love. If you are in fear, lift yourself up to The Divine. You can do this very easily and you can help others lift themselves up. You don't complicate issues. You are very clear about the direction in which to go. And it is helpful for you to follow this inner direction. These lyrics offer you hope. They offer you guidance. I sense you follow that guidance.

This song makes you happy, confident and courageous.

CHAPTER THIRTY-ONE

"Mayonnaise" performed by Smashing Pumpkins

If this is your favorite song, then you are probably special in these ways:

- Soft
- Intimate
- Gentle
- Have a yearning for…
- Intuitive and open to visions and dreams
- Think deeply
- Desire to express love
- A deeply emotional individual
- Open to higher guidance
- Creative
- Intellectual
- Compassionate and empathetic
- A sensitive spirit
- Poetic

Client: Jordan

It has been an absolute treat to intuit this Song Read for you. I had not heard this music before. What a wonderful song!

I interpret your deeper connection to the song in this way:

The soulful guitar sound connects you beautifully to Source. You are soft, intimate and gentle. There is a sense of longing in you. Your ajna, temple and crown chakras are very open. You are open to intuition, visions, fairies, angels, dreams and guidance. This music connects you to The Divine. This music is powerful for you.

You are an individual who thinks with depth and penetration. Like many of us, you have some wounds. And you want to let go and let these wounds heal. But you try to impose your will on the world. This blurs your vision, and prevents you from taking into consideration all points of view. I sense anger and hurt. The lyrics have meaning for you. There is sadness in you and also a desire to express love—to express profound, rollicking, full, overwhelming love.

You connect to all of the instruments being played here. The instruments express your range of emotions from the soft and subtle uptake of emotions to profound drowning emotions. You have probably been hurt in the past and you don't quite understand why. You are open to higher guidance. You are well supported by your guides (loving beings, such as ascended masters, guardian angels and spirit guides who exist on a higher spiritual plane) and angels. You may or may not be aware of them but they are here with you. Our guides love and support us. You don't walk alone in this world.

You are a soft, gentle, open and deeply emotional individual. You are also creative and intellectual. There are energetic tears in your eyes while I am intuiting this Song Read for you. Your pain and hurt are coming through. Time, forgiveness, openness and guidance will be your allies. And, of course, because you have experienced this pain and hurt, you have the benefit of compassion and empathy to share with your fellow companions in the human race.

The introduction in the song is beautiful and tender. You are a sensitive soul. I sense a redemptive quality. Of coming out of the shower and being cleansed in this sound. The lyrics are maybe autobiographical for you. You love these lyrics as they touch you so deeply. You love the poetry of the lyrics. You love the breadth of the lyrics. This song in many ways is a gift for you. It is so beautiful. These lyrics seem to express perfectly, beautifully, poetically, seriously, hurtfully, truthfully what pain can do to us. Thankfully we come out of our pain. Again, I have the image of emerging from the shower.

In the tarot, "The Fool" represents the spirit. He can be the foolish young man, not paying attention to where he is going, and he can also be a blank canvas, capable of spiritual enlightenment.

This combination of musical arrangements, voice, and lyrics is a wonderful combination for you. It brings you to Source. It carries you to The Divine. Follow the message of this song and you will find completion.

This is so beautiful for you. You are moved so much and touched so tenderly and deeply. The more you delve into your emotions the freer you are.

CHAPTER THIRTY-TWO

"My Way" performed by Frank Sinatra

If this is your favorite song, then you are probably special in these ways:

- Sincere
- Solemn and dignified
- Possess high values
- Confident
- Possess self-belief
- An upstanding member of the community
- Active and driven
- Dutiful
- Take responsibility for your life and do not play the victim role
- Romantic
- Overcome obstacles
- Optimistic
- Open to intuition
- Desire your contribution to life to mean something

Client: Tim

It has been a pleasure to intuit this Song Read for you.

I interpret the hidden messages in your favorite song in this way:

You are very sincere. You are also quite solemn and you possess high values. You like to uphold your values and you demonstrate these values. You are confident and you trust in yourself.

You are probably an upstanding member of the community, represented through the image of a suit and a tie. You present as a masculine personality, as in yang. You are active and driven rather than receptive and receiving. You have an active personality. But underneath your masculine exterior you appear to be a bit of a softie.

You are quite dutiful. You fulfill your duties and your responsibilities very well. And you are happy to assume these responsibilities. You take responsibility for your life. Women probably like you. You would be a good provider. The violin vibration brings out your romantic side.

The big music, where the music really sings in, connects you to Source and a sense of love. You feel a sense of greatness and you are aware that this greatness is a force bigger than you.

I sense that every time you get knocked down in life, you pick yourself up, dust yourself off, and off you go again. This is a great quality in you. You make me laugh a lot while you are doing this, so I sense that you see the fun side, the funny side to the hard knocks life gives you. In this way you are very optimistic.

You connect with this music beautifully. You have nice open upper chakras. Most of the energy is in the head and the crown chakra. You are open to intuition. You seem to be reserved with your emotions, though you do feel them. The louder aspect of the music and the rousing quality in the music seems to really grab your attention. This expresses for you the magnificence of life down here on the physical plane. The full orchestra sound sits very well with you. You want your contribution to life to mean something. You want to leave a mark, in some way, for people and your community.

The orchestral element helps you open your heart and it helps you to express yourself and acknowledge the help you have had. You express real emotion here.

The only thing you need to be careful of is to be mindful of arrogance. When you are very capable of being successful, and when you are prepared to take risks, other people can sometimes be jealous. So it is to your benefit to be humble and to show others how to manage and become a success. Since you understand success well, why not teach it? It is to your advantage to share your gift of easily being able to achieve goals and to teach others how to do this. Other people will benefit from this.

CHAPTER THIRTY-THREE

"No. 13 Baby" performed by The Pixies

If this is your favorite song, then you are probably special in these ways:

- Creative
- Intuitive
- An unusual character
- Appreciate intimacy
- Open-hearted
- Open to emotions
- Stand out and are different
- Express freely
- Courageous
- Authentic
- Have a sweet sense of humor
- Enjoy mystery

Client: Ed

It has been a pleasure to intuit this Song Read for you. I had not heard this music before.

I interpret your deeper connection to the song in this way:

You are connected to Source with this song. You are a creative individual and you enjoy the creative aspect of this music. The musical sound moves and connects you to Source and to other people.

Your upper chakras are very open. You are open to The Divine, to intuition, to creativity, to expression. You seem to be an unusual character and are sometimes misunderstood by others. Maybe this is because you present as different. You would like to be understood and you appreciate intimacy.

There is some confusion in your energy field. Maybe at times you talk without thinking beforehand or considering how your point of view will be received.

Your heart is open and you are a creative individual. You tend to work more from your emotions than through logic. You are open to your emotions and do not suppress them. I get the impression that you probably stand out. I am receiving the image of a punk rocker! Black hair and black clothes. You present as a much tougher person than you really are. And people probably look at you because of your difference. It is likely that others may be envious of the way you express freely. It can take enormous courage to express oneself authentically. You are comfortable with your own authenticity.

You have a sweet sense of humor. There is something sweet about you. Maybe you have been wounded in the past, but you still possess an element of authentic sweetness within you.

You have your own interpretation of what the lyrics mean for you. You enjoy the poetry of the lyrics and you enjoy the obscure elements of the lyrics. You do not always like things to be clear. You seem to enjoy the mystery held within people, within yourself and within lyrics. This music connects you to Source quite well.

I sense you are a creative soul, especially visually creative, and it would be worth exploring in more depth your creative side.

CHAPTER THIRTY-FOUR

"Once in a Life" performed by Kyau and Albert

If this is your favorite song, then you are probably special in these ways:

- Creative
- Have an affinity with chemistry and physics
- Opens to magic
- Enjoy sharing
- Naturally stop and smell the roses
- Aware of spiritual signposts
- Have a strong sense of smell
- Intellectual
- Aware of subtleties

Client: Lewis

It has been a pleasure to intuit this Song Read for you. I had not heard this music before.

When I was interpreting this song, I selected the dance track and it seemed to suit you perfectly. The dance version has a lot of techno sounds and your connection with this song is in those sounds. When I listen to the lyrics version, the music and the lyrics doesn't breathe in the same way. The music element is not so important in this version. I sense that the Song Read shown through the longer dance version of this music is about your potential. This longer version expresses your abstraction and creativity, your chemistry. This is not an accident that the Song Read is from two versions of the one song.

I interpret your deeper connection to this song in this way:

Extended dance mix version:

This dance mix expresses your potential, and you may be well on your way in many of these areas.

The electronic sound seems to represent neurons firing off. You appear to have an affinity with chemistry and physics. Then the sound becomes fuller and it goes right down into your lower abdomen. The sound helps you to opens up to the magic.

You have a beautiful, clear connection to Source. You possess a clear energy field. You are wonderfully creative. You can become quite lost in this sound, quite transported. You enjoy sharing this song with your friends.

It is possible that sometimes you find it difficult to express your intuitions. At times you find it a bit muffling and feel a bit ruffled trying to express some of the delightful qualities within you. You have a wonderful light in your aura. It is very clean, very luminous. This music absolutely brings you to Source. I can see you dancing to this music.

You enjoy the journey. You also enjoy the end goal. But you are happy to enjoy the journey and the process and you tend to be one of those individuals who smell the roses along the way. You see the spiritual signposts and enjoy them. Your sense of smell is probably quite pronounced.

Lyric version:

You tend to live mainly in your head, but not exclusively in the world of intellect. You are also open to intuition, to subtleties. The energy is within your head. I sense you are an intellectual person. If you are after more balance in life, consider activating the area of emotions through the heart chakra. This will help balance your intellect with intuition and emotions.

CHAPTER THIRTY-FIVE

"One" performed by U2

If this is your favorite song, then you are probably special in these ways:

- Loving
- Open to intuition
- Express emotions easily
- Joyful
- Feel a deep connection with all people
- Accept and appreciate others
- Protective
- Developing compassion
- Willing to feel emotions, both "good" and "bad"
- Intellectual
- Open to faith
- Aware of the spiritual law of "unity"—all is one
- Eager to help and support others
- A teacher

Client: Hayden

It has been an absolute treat to intuit this Song Read for you. What a wonderful song and sound!

I interpret the hidden messages in your favorite song in this way:

The predominant energy coming through for you is emotion, especially love. There is an ecstatic love here too. This song, the music and Bono's voice connect you to Source. Your crown chakra is open and your heart chakra is expressed through the meridians (traditional Chinese medicine channels of chi, or subtle life energy) in your arms. You desire to touch people and to hold people. Your forehead chakra is open. You are open to intuition.

You may at times be a slave to your emotions. This is not all bad, since emotions allow you to feel and experience life. There are energetic tears in your eyes. You feel deep love, joy, and connection with other people through this music. I also sense hurt here, and some of this hurt is still in your energy body (the subtle life energy system, aura and chakras that surround the physical body.) There is some energy congestion in your upper arms, which are connected to the heart chakra. So you are literally holding on to some of the hurt. You have been hurt both emotionally and intellectually. But when you try to figure it out rationally you can't make sense of it. This hurt is also a universal hurt, and connects you through the experience of pain to your friends and to the world at large. Be kind to yourself with this. The benefit of this pain, this hurt, is that you easily accept and appreciate others and desire to protect them from hurt. You are developing compassion.

On the whole you express your emotions well and they flow through your body easily. There is also an acceptance of emotion and a willingness to feel the emotions, both "good" and "bad." You may at times be ruled by your emotions, though you also present as quite balanced. Your intellectual side is also strong.

This song gives you a huge, colossal amount of faith. The faith coming through is very strong. You are very connected to Source. You and your higher soul are communing together here. Your soul and subconscious are speaking to you through this song.

There is a sense of an ideal here for you, a sense of a deep meaning of what life is about and what we are down here for. You have an awareness of the spiritual law of "unity"—all is one.

Look for guidance in the lyrics. The lyrics will have a profound meaning for you. The love in this song can be the love of friends and family, romantic love and spiritual love. You naturally take care to avoid blame and victim games, and this is to your credit. You feel unified with people. You like the idea of helping people, supporting people, protecting people, and seeing everybody as "a unified single force." You also comprehend that wherever you venture on planet Earth you will be met by friends and family. You have an ability to feel connected to all people.

I sense great pain in these lyrics for you. The understanding you have arrived at is that love is a great healer, and to forgive. You have emerged from "the shower" with great strength, compassion, empathy, as a teacher. You also appreciate The Collective. We all share the same monadic force (a direct particle of the force of God), the great Holy Spirit.

This song allows you to connect with The Divine, with The Divine of people who have loved you and with The Divine of people you love. It even allows you to connect with The Divine of people who have hurt you.

The word I am receiving for you is "gracious," to walk graciously through life.

Client Feedback

"It isn't often I say that someone knows me better than myself but obviously you do! Your interpretation of my song was so insightful, and in fact you pointed out things that were true about me that I hadn't thought of!!! Thank you so much for your thoughts—you made my day. Anyone will come away with a new perspective from this book."--Hayden

CHAPTER THIRTY-SIX

"Radar Love" performed by Golden Earring

If this is your favorite song, then you are probably special in these ways:

- Open to intuition
- Open to telepathy
- Detail-orientated
- Observant
- Fun
- Have a strong auditory faculty
- Adventurous
- Willing to stretch and challenge yourself
- Agile and possess quick reflexes
- Have helpful and healthful boundaries
- Have a quality of lightness within you
- Have a good sense of humor

Client: Stephen

It has been a pleasure to intuit this Song Read for you.

I interpret your deeper connection to the song in this way:

Your temple chakras are open. This shows that you are open to intuition, to your sixth sense and telepathy. The temple chakras are doorways to expanded awareness. The tempo seems to be a little bit confusing for you. You pay great attention to detail and you are observant.

There is a lot of fun in you. Your sense of hearing is very developed. You easily differentiate between the different qualities of sound within your environment. You also have an open energy field.

You enjoy the beat of this song and it connects you to Source. You like adventure. You like to stretch yourself to see what you can do, as in the case of a dare. You like speed and you are agile, and possess quick reflexes. You probably have a talent for judo and karate. You have helpful and healthful boundaries in place.

I sense you are not bogged down by your challenges. You can easily pick yourself back up and get moving. You don't become too upset and disheartened by struggles. You do not give challenges undue weight. There is lightness within you. This is a fabulous quality to possess.

I feel that you would enjoy playing along with your guitar, strutting on the floor and on your knees. You make me laugh a lot and you have an easy lightness about you. You possess a very good sense of humor.

The hidden message for you is to develop the gift of your sixth sense.

CHAPTER THIRTY-SEVEN

"Resurrection Fern" performed by Iron and Wine

If this is your favorite song, then you are probably special in these ways:

- Happy and content
- Feel deeply
- A sensitive individual
- Comfortable alone
- A secret romantic
- In harmony with nature and animals
- Wise
- Honest and value truth
- A calm and gentle spirit
- Loyal
- Appreciate and accept openness and vulnerability
- Considerate
- Creative and artistic
- Open to psychic energies
- Have an internal sense of goodness
- Humble

Client: Angus

It has been a pleasure to intuit this Song Read for you. I had not heard this music before.

I interpret your deeper connection to the song in this way:

You possess country values, happiness, and contentment. You feel deeply and you are a sensitive individual. You are a deep thinker. You are in your head more often than in your heart. You are a bit of a loner, you are comfortable in your own company, but you are also a secret romantic.

You like animals and you are connected with nature. You remind me of a bird. If you were an animal you would probably be a bird flying high. I see checked shirts. You like dogs. You are sometimes surprised by how human beings get on together and you find it a little bit disconcerting. You are not surprised in a naïve way, but in a spiritual way. You have the wisdom to understand that people often do not need to interact in the unconscious way that they do. It surprises you a bit that people talk and operate from their hidden motivations and agendas.

You like the outdoors and you feel in harmony with nature. You would probably like bushwalking and camping. Often nature understands you more than people do. You connect with animals. You find them more honest than people. Nature and animals are very much a necessary respite for you.

Your energy field is clear. You are an unassuming person, sensitive, calm and uncomplicated. There is an ease to you. I pick up somebody tall and slim, although more in your energy body than your physical body. You seem to have languid movements and body language. You honor good country values and practice these values. Truth is important to you and you are a loyal friend. When you are with people or in relationships, you appreciate openness, vulnerability and acceptance. You appreciate these qualities in people. You possess these qualities, they are within you too. Maybe you are still searching for some things, or something, in life, and there appears to be a little reticence to go out there and claim what is rightfully yours. Maybe there is a little too much shyness in you.

You illustrate simplicity, ease, comfort in life, soft gentleness, happiness, sharing, consideration and softness. You can be a tad cynical. You wish the world were a more humane place. There is a creative, artistic quality in you which is probably why you are attracted to these lyrics.

There is a soft, gentle, spiritual feel to you. Visions come to mind. You seem to be open to psychic energies. You have an internal sense of goodness, but you tend to keep private about these aspects and not share them with your friends. You spend quite a lot of time in thought and you enjoy solving problems in your head for your own satisfaction. You have no need to show the solution to anybody else and have no ego and attachment to it. Your ego seems to be well in check and you are a humble person. People feel very comfortable with you. They trust you easily because they sense an inner calmness of spirit and a lack of judgment from you.

You are a soft gentle spirit and the world needs you. Don't go anywhere!

CHAPTER THIRTY-EIGHT

"Roadhouse Blues" performed by The Doors

If this is your favorite song, then you are probably special in these ways:

- Happy
- Open to experimentation
- A rebel
- Fun
- Have conviction
- Sexy
- Defiant
- Strong
- Stand up for your rights and do not back down from a challenge
- Confident
- Magnetic and possess a lot of presence
- The life and soul of the party

Client: Jennifer

It has been a pleasure to intuit this Song Read for you.

I interpret your deeper connection to the song in this way:

I sense you smiling and happy. You like to have a good time and are open to experimentation. You love the instruments in this song, especially the harmonica. There is probably a rebel in you. The music suggests what has happened to you in life. This song connects you to your past history. The energy behind you is strong. Perhaps you are living and thinking too much in the past. It may be helpful to remember that you have a choice as to whether you concentrate on past events or choose to pay attention to the present day.

I sense there is great fun in you. You also have conviction. You display a very strong front. You are sexy. You seem to be very guarded with your emotions, as you have possibly been hurt in the past. Sometimes the big-picture vision can become clouded because you tend to interpret it from a historical perspective. It may be helpful to become aware of habitual thoughts which do not serve you and to replace these with helpful encouraging thoughts.

You enjoy the big sound of the guitar and harmonica. I sense the line "serves them right!" There is defiance here and this music helps you to explain this defiance. You are a strong woman. You possess a lot of presence. You stand up for your rights and you do not back down from a challenge. You assert yourself with ease and confidence.

This music would work well with beer! You seem to be very much in the physical realm. You are very magnetic. You can easily influence people.

It is possible that you have issues with money, rejection or security.

Throughout this song, there appears to be a desire for the sound to take over and block out your normal day-to-day existence. You like to have a good time and your friends like you. You are often the life and soul of the party.

CHAPTER THIRTY-NINE

"Run Away" performed by Live

If this is your favorite song, then you are probably special in these ways:

- Intuitive
- Open to telepathy and clairvoyance
- Feel deeply
- Passionate
- Sensitive to the circumstances of others
- Express emotions easily
- Open-hearted
- Tend to stand by your convictions
- Stand up for people
- A good friend
- Desire love
- Welcoming and embracing
- Gentle
- Open to bliss

Client: Emily

I have enjoyed interpreting this Song Read for you. I had not heard this music before.

I interpret your deeper connection to the song in this way:

It very much feels as if you are in the room with me! You are very open to other worlds and intuition. You could well be telepathic or clairvoyant. You feel deeply and passionately. You are connected to spirit. There is some confusion for you in the astral realm (the realm of mind and thoughts). You appear to be highly intuitive and sensitive and you pick up a lot of energy from other people and what they are thinking. This confuses you.

You express your emotions easily and it is likely that you are guided by your emotions. You are happy to chase ultimate love. You are open-hearted and operate from your heart rather than your head. You emote easily and feel deeply.

You stand by your convictions. I also sense that you would support anybody who is being mistreated, someone not being allowed to state their case. You stand up for people. You are a good friend in this way.

You want love in your life. Love raises you. This song may allude to higher love, of love for The Divine and wanting to be in that realm. You may also have been hurt in love.

There is ease, and welcomeness, and gentleness, an embracing element to the guitar sound. These qualities are also within you. The music stirs you and it allows you to feel and express your emotions easily. You feel connected to others through this music. There is bliss here for you. The opening guitar riffs bring you a sense of the whole world coming together and loving together.

Beautiful!

Client Feedback

"Hi Awen,

You are spot on with saying I can't sit by and let others be mistreated. I am very much a voice (and really I'd guess also a force to be reckoned with) on behalf of the underdog. I can't help it. Sometimes it ends up costing me a lot emotionally and also takes time, and in some cases even money,- but it's like I have this unstoppable compulsion to make the world balanced again and have the wrongs righted even if they don't have any-thing to do with me.

I guess I could share a few stories.

A neighbor's little dog escaped her yard and was taken to the pound. The dog wasn't micro-chipped or de-sexed so it was go-ing to be a fortune for the lady to get her dog back, and every day that passed the cost went up an extra $80. My neighbor was so upset because she was broke and was terrified she would lose her dog. She could not see a way out of her mess. I guess it's when people lose all hope I just can't sit back and have them upset,- so I went on a mission to raise several hundred dollars within a few hours. I pawned some of my neighbor's stuff on her behalf, hit my boss up for a little advance, and called in some debts owed to me, and then finally I stood at the butcher's trading meat vouchers for cash (that my neighbor had won at the raffles) to customers who came to buy meat. Every-one else who has heard this story has cringed in embarrassment, and there's no way my neighbor would have done it, but I was determined that little dog was coming home that day. I sold off all the meat vouchers and sprung the dog from the pound that afternoon.

You are right about me having been hurt. For me the subject of unconditional love has been confusing and that kind of love it-self has been somewhat absent in my life.

You are also right about confusion for me when it comes to the astral realm.

I will leave a mark on this world. Maybe not a big one like the way famous people might, but instead it's all the little things I do. I hope that when I get to whatever magical number of good things I do then I will be at peace and feel whole."

Emily

CHAPTER FORTY

"Seven Wonders" performed by Fleetwood Mac

If this is your favorite song, then you are probably special in these ways:

- A talented individual
- Joyful
- Expressive
- Logical
- Open-hearted
- Sensitive
- Protective
- Loving
- Appreciate beauty
- Intuitive
- A balanced personality
- Have a magical quality within you
- Imaginative
- Potential for artistic and creative talents

Client: Isobel

It has been a pleasure to intuit this Song Read for you.

I interpret your deeper connection to the song in this way:

You have an abundant array of qualities to work, live, create and express with. You are a talented person.

Stevie Nicks' voice seems to make you rise up in a spiral. You feel great joy and you express great joy through this song. I see your hands over your heart and you are very expressive with your arms.

Your logical side can at times push out and overtake your emotional side. There is some darting around in the ajna chakra through the temples. There may be some confusion with the big picture of your life, indecision, such as "Am I in or am I out?" You may experience difficulty deciding which way to go. On occasion you may lack commitment and determination. This area seems to be a bit confusing for you. My impression of this is because you feel the pull of your head, your heart, and also your intuition. This may at times lead to indecision and internal conflict.

You have an open heart, but you are often ruled by your head.

You are sensitive and easily hurt. So your habitual response may be to protect yourself.

You love to express pure joy. Joy seems to be the highlight of life for you. This joy spreads out through your whole body and energy field. Your upper chakras shine with luminous light when this happens to you, and this is no mean feat. The beat of this music helps you to connect with your joy. You feel an abundant sense of love with this sound.

You like rainbows and love beauty and your intuitive side is open as well.

Your ajna chakra is activated. The lyrics seem to give you a sense of ideal. A sense of something you want to find in life. A goal, a direction. These lyrics are quite important to you.

You have a balanced personality. Your faculties, your heart and your head, are quite balanced. This music connects you to Source. The lyrics seem to transport you. The sound has a fairy-tale-like quality, a dream-like quality. You like the sound of the drums at the beginning of the music. It is as if they are preparing you to get ready to go somewhere. There is a magical quality here, and something in your imagination is unleashed through the merging of the voice, the music and especially the drum, which connects you more than the other sounds or the lyrics. The drums have a magical hold on you. This magical quality is also within you.

This sound activates all of your upper chakras, from heart upwards to crown. I see you dancing and swaying to this music and singing along to this song. It captures your imagination. You probably have a strong imagination. You may be artistic and creative too. Or perhaps you have the ability to be creative, but you choose not to express these talents. Perhaps you feel more comfortable expressing your rational side.

You love Stevie Nicks' distinctive voice. You appreciate the emotional aspect of her voice and connect to her voice exceedingly well.

Client Feedback

"Hi Awen,

Wow very interesting stuff. Most of what you said I was able to relate to very well. I'm sure there is plenty of truth in this reading, amazingly accurate in the earlier part of the reading. Happy to have taken part, it was very interesting. Thank you again for the pleasure of taking part."

Isobel

CHAPTER FORTY-ONE

"Sitting on the Dock of the Bay" performed by Otis Redding

If this is your favorite song, then you are probably special in these ways:

- Happy and content
- Soulful
- Gentle
- Optimistic
- Easy-going
- Possess a high level of the virtue "acceptance"
- Comfortable in the world of emotions
- Forgiving
- Empathetic
- Nurturing
- Support others
- Receptive
- Patient
- Have faith in the benevolence of The Divine

Client: Casey

I have enjoyed interpreting this Song Read for you.

I interpret your deeper connection to the song in this way:

These are the images which come to mind: the sun (the giver of life), hope, ease, a powerful and soulful voice, and an easy sense of flow.

You appear to be a happy, contented and a soulful person. You possess an easy and gentle nature. The whistling is sweet. You are happy and optimistic. You are an easy-going person.

There may be an autobiographical element in this song for you. You may already be aware of this. You possess a high level of the virtue "acceptance."

Water connects you to The Divine. In astrology, water is the element of our emotions. You emote easily and are comfortable in the world of emotions and the higher qualities of the heart, such as forgiveness and empathy. The astrological sign Cancer comes to mind— accepting, nurturing, supporting and emoting. You display the feminine and you are receptive, (to the good in life,) as in yin.

I sense that any loneliness you may feel, or may have felt in the past, is due to your individual and   different interpretation of life. You seem to have an acceptance of life. You understand the yin of life. You comprehend that life is naturally going to change around you and you will eventually arrive where you want to be. You feel no need to go out and make life change. Because this interpretation of life runs against the prevailing wisdom, you may feel lonely. But you are comfortable being more yin than yang. I sense you have a much stronger feminine, receptive energy (yin) than a masculine energy (yang).

You understand that we become far too involved in life. Life is really just an ebb and flow, an easy ebb and flow. You display great patience. I sense you have ultimate faith in the benevolence of The Divine. Despite any troubles you have encountered, I think you have learned to have faith. You display a higher awareness of The Divine

CHAPTER FORTY-TWO

"Slide Away" performed by Oasis

If this is your favorite song, then you are probably special in these ways:

- Possess depth of personality
- Comfortable with emotions
- Upbeat
- A happy spirit
- Practical
- Drawn to a sense of awe
- Open to revelation
- Have an understanding of spirituality
- Passionate and joyful
- Gifted at and content in relationships
- Possess an air of freshness
- Have secret wishes and dreams

Client: Jesse

It has been a pleasure to intuit this Song Read for you.

I interpret your deeper connection to the song in this way:

You possess depth and emotion. You have an upbeat personality. You are also a happy spirit who lives in the practical realm of the world. But this also means living in the limitations of the Maya (Sanskrit word meaning the illusion we call life, a veiling of the true self) of the practical world. You would like more euphoria in your life. And a word and virtue which really attracts you is "awe." You are open to revelation, to something bigger than yourself, an energy force bigger than yourself, but you haven't really come across this yet. The lyrics have a special meaning for you. You have some understanding of spirituality. Dreams can be an indicator for you, a precursor to what you are manifesting in life. So it may be a good idea to journal your dreams upon wakening.

You like the sunshine. You are passionate. You would love to run down the street, or on the beach, holding hands with somebody. You would enjoy the momentum, exhilaration and the freedom of this expression. I see you holding hands with somebody and this is joyful for you. The chakras in the hands are connected to the heart chakra, and so, ultimately, holding hands is joining heart chakras. You are happy with, gifted at and content in relationships. The astrological sign of Libra comes to mind: the sharing quality, the ease of relationship and the general ease of your personality.

You would probably also enjoy dancing to this music. Maybe, if you are a guitarist, you might strum along, too. I think you would enjoy the movement of this music. You like music and musical instruments. Incidentally, I think you would also enjoy a playful, physical mudslide! You would perhaps experience great fun rolling in a playful mudslide!

This music allows you to escape from life for a while. Listening to this song frees you inwardly. It may serve you to lose yourself inwardly and freely more often.

You have an air of freshness about you, with a hint of a secret passionist. But you hold this secret within you. You have secret wishes and dreams, but you don't share them easily.

There is an anthem-like quality at the beginning of this song. You would enjoy being with a mutually-inclusive group, a smallish group. A group of six would probably suit you well.

You seem to have the personality of someone dark-haired. And possibly you may even look like one of the members of this band?

CHAPTER FORTY-THREE

"Soul to Squeeze" performed by Red Hot Chili Peppers

If this is your favorite song, then you are probably special in these ways:

- Interesting
- Unusual and unorthodox
- Gentle
- Desire peace
- Aware of the subtleties in life
- Aware of the hidden undercurrents and motivations of human behavior
- Receptive to illusion
- Intuitive
- Have a good sense of humor
- Appreciate the absurd and the abstract
- Creative
- A deep thinker
- Aware of The Divine
- Drawn to love and desire love
- Accepting of the foibles and idiosyncrasies of others
- Feel deeply

Client: Brad

I have enjoyed intuiting this Song Read for you.

I interpret your deeper connection to the song in this way:

These are interesting and unusual sounds. There is gentleness, a gentle riff. These are qualities you also possess. You connect to the lyrics. You connect to Spirit. You desire peace. You are aware of the subtleties in life and the hidden undercurrents and motivations of human behavior. You are connected to your higher soul. You are open and receptive to illusion and your intuition. You are also interesting, unorthodox and gentle.

You have a sense of humor and enjoy the absurd in life. You appreciate the absurd and the abstract. You are also a creative individual.

The opening sequence of the song and the beginning guitar riffs seem to have a sense of home and family to them for you. They appear to point to your early childhood.

You are a deep thinker and pensive and you are very aware of the world of Spirit and of The Divine. I sense confusion within you as to whether or not to follow your higher guidance. Your intuition is strong and I think you may sometimes be hard on yourself when you don't follow your intuition; but be gentle with yourself, and remember that most of us also don't follow our intuition all of the time.

You possibly have had pain in your life, like many of us, and this has made you ponder the deeper and darker elements of existence. Also you are drawn to love and desire love, especially a deep spiritual love. But maybe you don't feel confident that this kind of love is attainable in this life (even though, of course, it is). Meditation would suit you. It can help free you and give you peace of mind. You seem to be accepting but also cynical. You are very accepting of the foibles and idiosyncrasies of others.

An interesting element in this music is that the sound of the guitar is languid and easy. The paradox is that this is not how you feel deep down. The addition of the drums, the crashing drums, the chaos and destruction in the middle of the song, seems to indicate the split within you. You would like to have a naïve interpretation of life but you are conscious of the deeper elements. You understand that good and bad belong to the same spectrum, they are just different expressions and at different ends of the same spectrum. You comprehend that good and bad co-exist. You understand pain and pleasure. You probably savor your pain to some extent, as you tend to feel deeply. The music and the lyrics are a great dichotomy, with one easy-flowing and the other alluding to the darker aspects within human nature. You understand this dichotomy is within all of us. Peace is going to be of benefit to you.

You have a gentle smile.

CHAPTER FORTY-FOUR

"Stairway to Heaven" performed by Led Zeppelin

If this is your favorite song, then you are probably special in these ways:

- Have a yearning for…
- Interesting
- Open to emotions
- Empathetic
- Intuitive and understand the spiritual world
- The searcher and the traveler
- Drawn to awe, magnificence and splendor
- The Creative artist
- Gentle and serene
- Happy and feel at home in nature and all of the weather elements
- Reverent and profound
- Understand mythology and symbology
- Articulate, talented at communication and a storyteller
- Intelligent
- Reflective and considerate
- Fluid and able to flow throughout life easily

Client: Mitchell

I have thoroughly enjoyed intuiting this Song Read for you. Thank you for this special choice.

I interpret your deeper connection to the song in this way:

There is sadness and longing in the guitar sound at the beginning of this song. A sense of ritual. A sense of storytelling. A sense of somebody turning over the pages to tell us a story, a parable. And the storyteller could indeed be The Pied Piper, from the fable. Some of this sadness, longing and a touch of regret are in you too.

The instruments are interesting. The wind instruments have a somber, melancholy lament to them. Conversely, the strings are uplifting and here we are rising up into the whole story, the magnificence. The fullness of the story is coming through now. This is great storytelling. You are open to your emotions. You are open to your feelings and have empathy because you've overcome your own challenges. You are open to your intuition. You understand the spiritual world and you are connected to Source.

There seems to be an epic quality to this music. You can be the wanderer, the searcher, the traveler. And you are amazed at the awe, magnificence and the splendor you find.

The sounds combine to paint a golden color. Amazing as this sounds, the music seems to paint a color. I perceive that this is subtle and in the background. Your crown chakra and temple chakras are open and you are connected to The Divine. You are wide open to this song. It connects you easily. You are very open to intuition and spirit.

There is a little bit of confusion with your logical approach. You are probably a right-brain, creative, gentle, intuitive type of soul, and maybe you get a bit lost in the world of logic and reason, which is how we are brought up in school. So perhaps you struggled at school. Also there appears to be some confusion and getting caught up in the Maya. You know the Maya is not real.

You appear to be happy in all of the weather elements. You seem to have a deeper meaning attached to each of these elements—a private meaning as to what they mean for you. You are happy and feel at home in nature. The electric guitar almost sounds like ringing bells.

The music then changes again on the journey and this illustrates the journey all of us go through. We don't travel one straight path. We go up and down hills, winding roads, traveling at different tempos. So this song and the music seem to be a great example of our journey down here on Earth. Even the screeching voice section is really clear. It makes me think of an older, crooked-face woman, like the witch in Snow White. She is pointing out Snow White.

There is great reverence in you. You understand mythology and probably symbology. You are aware of the subtleties in the English language and converse with a high degree of articulation. You comprehend these lyrics deeply. You are talented at communication, writing, reading, public speaking etc. This song and these lyrics help express the subtleties, pureness, sereneness of you. There are soft subtleties here. You are highly intelligent, highly creative and highly intuitive, reflective and considerate. You are probably able to use words in a beautiful way and appreciate good literature. The creative artist is within you.

You are profound and you are drawn to the higher calling of these lyrics. It is possible that you are looking for the wonderment of The Divine. You understand the importance of experiencing awe and amazement. But maybe there are some challenges and trial and tribulations before arriving here, as there are for many of us.

It feels like a coming-of-age song and ritual. You connect very deeply to these lyrics. This song has probably helped you out quite a lot. Many blessings come to us on the breeze. They glide in easily, gently, they don't seem to arrive with a fanfare and I think you are aware of this.

I sense a magnum opus within you. This song is so big in its range, its diversity and its message. It is actually quite difficult to take an individual person from this song because of the sense of collectivity with this song. The electric guitar toward the end seems to express a wholeness of where we are all going.

You are a wonderful, gentle, fluid soul and you know where to go to find Heaven. The word "fluid" expresses you. You seem to have the capacity, at times, to express yourself as a stream of golden silk.

I wish you joy and a plentiful knapsack on your journey. Blessings.

CHAPTER FORTY-FIVE

"Stay" performed by Rihanna

If this is your favorite song, then you are probably special in these ways:

- Open to feelings
- Possess clarity
- Express yourself easily and clearly
- Forthright
- Feel deeply
- Empathetic and compassionate
- Passionate
- Have a big beautiful heart
- Generous
- Peaceful
- Loving and joyful
- Appreciative and grateful
- Persistent
- Connected to the Earth

Client: Chloe

It has been a pleasure to intuit this Song Read for you. I had not heard this music before.

I interpret your deeper connection to the song in this way:

You are very open to your feelings. You like Rihanna's voice. I sense a spiritual interpretation to this music. You possess a lot of clarity. You connect to The Divine. You express yourself very easily and clearly. You are probably quite forthright in your expression. You seem to be ruled by your heart and your emotions. You feel deeply. You also have empathy and compassion for people.

You love the deep vocal way Rihanna sings the lyrics. You love the depth and the passion of this.

I sense there is a spiritual element in these lyrics for you. This is where the message for you lies. You have a big beautiful heart which activates very easily. You express the qualities of the heart: generosity, compassion, peace, love, joy, appreciation and gratitude. You have deep passion within you and you seem to be very much ruled by your feelings. The strength of your feelings tells you how intense life is for you.

This music connects you to Source easily. For you, the persistency of the piano sound seems to hold a resonance. It is possible that you are very persistent too! This song also connects you to love and to beautiful feelings of love, fullness, wholeness and unity. You have wonderfully open chakras, particularly from the heart to the crown. You are very connected through the heart. I sense the deep message for you is hidden in your emotional connection to the lyrics. Especially the lyrics in a spiritual context. Maybe the love you are looking for is spiritual love. There is an almost baptismal quality to the piano playing, playing and playing.

This song, the piano sound and the clarity of the lyrics really fall into step with you. The reason I am using these specific words is because this affects your energy field in your legs. It grounds you down here on Earth. This sense of love you feel grounds you and connects you to Earth.

You have deep love within you. I have received the word "pure" for you. Something perhaps which you aspire to. You have a lot of clarity in you and the color white is a nice match for you too. Beautiful connection

CHAPTER FORTY-SIX

"Sultans of Swing" performed by Dire Straits

If this is your favorite song, then you are probably special in these ways:

- Happy
- Groovy, have a natural inner rhythm and move gracefully
- Accept circumstances and others easily
- Likable
- Magnetic
- Gentle, open and receptive
- At ease within yourself
- Undemanding
- Honest
- Tactful and diplomatic
- Considerate
- Assertive
- Have a good sense of humor
- Graceful and charming
- Balance weaving together work, rest and play
- A free bird

Client: Oliver

It has been an absolute treat to intuit this Song Read for you.

I interpret the hidden messages in your favorite song in this way:

The guitar sound in this music makes you happy. You are quite a "groovy" person. You have grace in your movements. You appear to be very languid. You have an ease about you and you are very accepting. You connect with your friends with great ease. And you are very likable.

People genuinely like you and this happens with very little effort on your part. You are magnetic and people are pulled to you. There is a gentleness in you which people like, but you are not really concerned what other people think about you. This is one of your great strengths and this is one of the reasons why people like you. Many people would like to count you as a friend.

You are very undemanding, honest and tactful. You are diplomatic, considerate and also assertive, but not overly so. You have a good sense of humor. I can see you dancing to this music. People would like to dance with you because you have an easy way on the dance floor. You know how to move to music. You have an uncomplicated, graceful, charming manner, but this is not over the top, it comes from within you. This is not an image you put on for the outside world, it's the real you.

You know how to go out and enjoy yourself. You are not excessive, but you are not overly moderate either. You seem to have a good understanding of the precise dose to take with all of your activities. So you are balanced with weaving together work, rest and play. You enjoy the pace of this music and it seems to represent the pace of how you live your life, which would probably be at a measured pace, a balanced pace. "Rhythm" is a word that suits you.

You are open and receptive. You are very connected to Source. You are connected through your antakarana, from crown, down through your body to Earth. You have an effortless sense of connection with everybody around you as well.

You are free. You have an inner free bird inside. This is your magnetism.

The guitar riffs sit very well in your energy field. You like the sensitivity of the sound of the strings. The guitar sounds express you very well. Your imagination and inner sensitivity are captured when the guitar sounds becomes quicker and higher. You have a natural inner rhythm. You display quite a lot of harmony but others don't always see this in you. You are equally happy by yourself, with a small group of intimate friends or with a large group. You are at ease in relationships, and this is because you are at ease within yourself. I bet you're also a good storyteller.

It is very hard not to like you. I'd like to have you as a friend too!

Client Feedback

"Thanks Awen!

I'm surprised you can glean so much from a song but I think you're pretty spot on. Let me know if you're doing something similar later on."

Oliver

CHAPTER FORTY-SEVEN

"Sundown Syndrome" performed by Tame Impala

If this is your favorite song, then you are probably special in these ways:

- Possess a lot of energy
- Happy
- Expectant
- Passionate and whole-hearted
- Artistic, creative and imaginative
- Secure in yourself
- Assertive
- Enjoy moving to music
- Expressive
- Big-hearted and joyful
- Accept others and circumstances easily
- Have a good voice
- Curious
- At home with your five senses

Client: Natalie

I have so enjoyed intuiting this Song Read for you. I was not familiar with this song.

I interpret your deeper connection to the song in this way:

You have a lot of energy and you are happy, encompassing, expectant, sailing smoothly through life. You are also passionate, wholehearted, artistic and creative, imaginative and secure in yourself. You are assertive and secure in your opinions and beliefs.

I sense energetic swelling around the middle abdomen. Maybe you are pregnant or maybe you are giving birth to new ideas and creativity.

This music is expansive for you. And this music raises you to Spirit. You enjoy moving to this music. Movement and music seem to go together for you. You are expressive. I sense you dancing like a ballerina, with your arms in the air, big-hearted, open and accepting. I sense you pirouetting with one leg bent at the knee. You have an open posture, encompassing all that is, accepting all that is. You have a wide smile, open arms and there is joy in you. Music is a gesture for you.

You possess a strong throat chakra. You have a good voice and you are expressive, but, paradoxically, you also seem to have some issues with expression. Often our greatest talent is also the area of our greatest fear and it is likely that you swallow words without expressing them. Also, your communication can at times be reactive rather than smooth. Occasionally you can over-think situations, and you may experience frustration at the limitations of words, preferring emotion, movement and the abstract.

The music combinations are exciting for you. There is some curiosity for you here. You seem to enjoy and derive great pleasure from the mixing and blending of sounds. You probably also possess a sophisticated palate, and the fusion of intense, sublime tastes give you pleasure. You are at home with all of your senses: audio, visual appreciation of beauty, sensual touch from massage. Your sense of smell is refined too. I perceive that you would derive enormous pleasure from assimilating the senses and allowing one sense to move easily into the flow of the others. This indicates artistic and creative talents.

I perceive a very feminine energy. The planet/goddess Venus comes to mind.

CHAPTER FORTY-EIGHT

"Sunshine" performed by Old Man River

If this is your favorite song, then you are probably special in these ways:

- Possess an upbeat personality
- Interested in the deeper meaning of life
- Value simplicity
- Possess well-developed instincts
- Have faith
- Optimistic
- Joyful
- Aware of the spiritual law of unity—all is one
- Spiritual
- Enjoy the abstract and the unusual
- Generous
- Aware of the mass consciousness

Client: Simon

I have thoroughly enjoyed intuiting this Song Read for you. I had not heard this music before.

I interpret your deeper connection to the song in this way:

You have an upbeat personality and display an upbeat tempo. "The sun" is the giver of life. You enjoy getting into the groove of the music and the deeper meaning of life. There is a beautiful deep groove to the music that makes you want to move and become lost within the music, to blend in with the sound. The music extends into the dimensions of meditation and dance. The simplicity of the lyrics offers higher guidance for all of us. We can make life so complicated and miss the deep inner meaning. You have very well-developed instincts. You have faith and are an optimistic individual.

The song appears to be in your head. You are listening through the head. This song is perhaps an ideal for you. This music contains great joy and this joy is also within you. There is almost a gospel riff and an anthem quality to the music. You understand that we are all linked together as one. This song is probably a form of gospel for you. I think the meaning for you is spiritual, not religious. You are possibly a very spiritual person.

The light is also important for you. The Divine brings light to dispel the darkness. The sun also brings light. You agree with the sentiment of the song. The music has Indian sitar sounds, and India is the home to so many gurus and spiritual guides.

The repetition of the lyrics and music and the simplicity of the sound seem to enhance the spiritual message. Repetition and simplicity are often used in Sanskrit chants and this helps us to meditate and move into other realms more easily.

You enjoy the abstract and the unusual in life. I receive the idea of people wanting to clap and join in. You are generous and value the ideal of sharing.

You are aware of the mass consciousness of life all around you

CHAPTER FORTY-NINE

"Taro" performed by Alt J

If this is your favorite song, then you are probably special in these ways:

- Intellectual
- Inventive
- A scientist
- Connect with the world's heart
- A unique individual
- Adaptable
- Joyful
- Wish good things for the world
- Appreciate beauty, harmony and depth
- Open to ambiguity
- Gentle
- Possess camaraderie
- Poet
- Understand that through badness, good things come
- Counselor
- Attracted to the abstract

Client: Marcus

Thank you for the opportunity to intuit this Song Read for you. I had not heard this music before.

I interpret your deeper connection to the song in this way:

The visions I receive are of nature, trees, leaves, sunlight. There is a wonderful voice, an ethereal voice from other realms.

I think that you are intellectual. You have an inventive quality in you. There is a bit of a scientist here. I can almost see somebody in a white lab coat mixing ingredients with steam rising from the concoction! There is a bit of that Einstein, white-frizzy-haired quality about you. Here is the "mad scientist" interpretation of the music. It is lovely. The music is more in your head than your heart. Your heart is there, but the head space takes precedence for you. And with your heart, it is not about yourself, it's about connecting with the world and the world's heart rather than your own singular heart. You are a unique individual. The song and the music connect to your uniqueness, to your adaptability, and, in many ways, to many people, many things and many experiences.

The carnival sounds are beautiful. I'm receiving the impression of an Indian sound coming together in joy. This type of Indian music is joyous and it allows all of your connections to come together and whirl together. This is very uplifting. It's like gentle gospel music. You wish good things for the world. Your mind is not solely focused on yourself.

The beauty in this song is easy to see. The harmony, depth and emotion of the music and the soft swaying movement, rising up to the heavens—it's easy to see why this is your favorite song!

The song is showing other things, too: ambiguity, chameleon characteristics. These qualities are also in you.

There is some heavy energy on my left shoulder, the left arm. I am not sure why. I think of a gunshot. Yes, it's a gunshot with a bullet in the upper arm. It may be possible that you have been a soldier in a past life.

There is gentleness to you. There is a camaraderie in you. The poetry of the words has a deep impact on you. You understand the lyrics. You understand that humanity can be beautiful and also not beautiful.

It can be violent, it can be destructive, it can be beautiful and it can be everything. But ultimately it all joyously rises to the ultimate reality of spirit. You have an understanding that through badness, good things come. Through apparent wrongdoing, through apparent pain, redemption is gained. You understand this. You have the ability to counsel others who are in pain.

You, my friend, are attracted to the abstract. You like art. Cryptic clues intrigue you and you are good at solving problems from these clues as well.

Welcome!

Client Feedback

"Wow! Your analysis was really fantastic and accurate. The way you analyze music is very interesting and admirable for me, a writer, a musician and a person. What you've written not only applies to me but also the song. The song is about a war photographer Gerda Taro and her relationship with Robert Capa. It's very interesting if you can get past the guy's interesting vocal style and make out his lyrics. I'm seeing this band in July and this analysis will make their performance even more special.

Regards and Thanks,"

Marcus

CHAPTER FIFTY

"The Rain Song" performed by Led Zeppelin

If this is your favorite song, then you are probably special in these ways:

- Possess a strong bond with Spirit
- A nurturer, soft and enabling
- Open hearted and in touch with emotions
- Intuitive and ethereal
- Imaginative and open to possibilities
- Loving and joyful
- Give and share easily
- Appreciative
- Forgiving
- Soothe troubled souls
- Reverent
- Open to magic
- Accept that there is a reason for everything which happens
- Balanced in yin and yang energy
- Intellectual
- Know yourself well

Client: Alexa

It has been an absolute honor to intuit this Song Read for you. I had not heard this music before. What a beautiful song!

I interpret your deeper connection to the song in this way:

You have an exceptionally strong bond with Spirit. It seems as if the energy of the music wraps you up in a warm blanket. It cocoons you, nurtures you and is soft and enabling. You also possess these delightful qualities. The musical energy is strong in your arms, especially the upper arms. The chakras in the arms are connected to the heart chakra, so this represents an open heart. As your heart chakra opens, so does your crown chakra, wide and full. This indicates that you are very open to The Divine, Spirit, intuition, imagination, love, joy, giving, sharing, appreciation and forgiveness. This song is an easy and natural way for you to connect with these qualities in yourself. You like to nurture and to hold, and can easily soothe troubled souls.

The musical interlude in the song is very special to you. This music expresses your imaginative gifts and your openness to possibilities. These expressions are special for you and you hold these qualities with reverence, in tender cupped hands. I sense magic in this song for you, especially in the full orchestra section. It mirrors your conception of all that is: awe, bliss, swaying, and tears of joy.

The fairy tale "Jack and the Beanstalk" comes to mind—climbing up the tendrils into the reality of another world.

The energy of tears appears in you. This is perhaps a recurring theme with your favorite music. Maybe you sometimes listen to this song when you are sad or something has not worked out as you had wanted. This music uplifts you and provides you with ultimate security in spirit. You accept that there is a reason for everything which happens to you. This song is a refuge for you. You understand how all of life is interconnected, and when you are not in touch with this ultimate truth, you experience sadness.

Sometimes there is an excessively strong determination in you. But you have the ability to master this.

This music shows that you are balanced in yin and yang energy. You feel equally at home in intellect and intuition. It is likely that you work with your intellect as a means to express this other side of yourself. The energy is strongest in your arms, indicating that you probably work with your hands. You have within you an ethereal quality, a sensitivity and lightness. Water appears visually in this Song Read, showing that you emote easily and are in touch with your emotions. You are happy to run the gamut of all emotions, including emotions that plumb the depths.

You enjoy poetry and fineness and refinement. There are not too many surprises here. You know yourself well but seek confirmation.

A mantra that might appeal to you is: "Divine I am."

"Cosmic" is a word you may like.

CHAPTER FIFTY-ONE

"The Story of my Life" performed by Social Distortion

If this is your favorite song, then you are probably special in these ways:

- Possess an upbeat personality
- Have faith
- Resilient and have the ability to overcome challenges and make progress
- Have a good sense of timing
- Like being outdoors
- Desire to be happy and carefree
- Shy
- A unique individual
- Developing self-worth and self-love
- Have the capacity to dream big
- Genuinely like people
- Introspective

Client: Cooper

Thank you for the opportunity to intuit this Song Read for you. I had not heard this music before.

I interpret your deeper connection to the song in this way:

This is an upbeat song. You have faith in the world. The beat of the music shows your ultimate faith and resilience. You accept both the good and bad, and because of this, you have the ability to move on from challenges and make progress. You have a good sense of timing. You can at times sense the ultimate joy in life. You like being outdoors. You want to be happy and carefree. You like to have the wind in your hair. You connect to the lyrics easily; maybe the biography of the song mirrors your own experience. You are shy, a bit hidden, and you prefer to keep private rather than step forward into the limelight.

You were brought up to be a good person, but now you are probably questioning all of the "shoulds" in your life. This can be very helpful. The "shoulds" have the ability to harness you. It is better to break free from these constraints.

You are a unique individual, but maybe you have not received a lot of reassurance and confirmation of this fact. Perhaps your goal is to transform by focusing on good feelings, to uncover the gems within you—confidence, strength and courage. And also acceptance, love and respect of yourself and your innate lovability. If you focus on nurturing yourself, you will free yourself from other people's expectations.

You have the capacity to dream big, but maybe not understand that these big dreams are actually possible. Perhaps you did not have a role model to demonstrate this aspect of fulfilling your dreams. I sense a learning opportunity here. If you focus on nurturing yourself, you will open up the possibility of your dreams coming to fruition through persistence, belief and action.

You genuinely like people and you like being with your friends. You have an upbeat personality, but you balance this with some introspection. You like community. You enjoy mutual feeling and sharing of emotions, ideas and concepts.

CHAPTER FIFTY-TWO

"Time Goes By" performed by The Spice Girls

If this is your favorite song, then you are probably special in these ways:

- Express love
- A sweet little gem!
- Allow other people to be themselves and accept all that happens in life
- Value harmony
- Joyful
- Appreciative
- A happy spirit
- Understand eternity and are in tune with fate and destiny
- Soft
- Fascinated by the concepts of soul love
- Share easily
- In touch with your feelings
- Have a vision full of harmony, openness, appreciation and flow
- See the beauty in life

Client: Lucy

It has been a pleasure to intuit this Song Read for you. I had not heard this music before.

I interpret your deeper connection to the song in this way:

You easily express love. You are a sweet little gem! You are well connected to Source and to other people. You allow other people to be themselves and their minor flaws do not irritate you. Harmony is important to you. You have a lot of joy and much appreciation for all that you have in life and all that you have been given. You are very connected with Spirit.

You do not have many hidden motives in life. This is a rare quality. I sense you are young and move through life without too many hiccups.

I have a big smile on my face intuiting this Song Read for you. You are a happy soul! I see someone reaching up and outwards. You have a deep understanding of eternity. When The Sydney Harbour Bridge had the word "Eternity" emblazoned on it, it almost seemed set up for you! You are soft, and open to fate, destiny and sharing. You are intrigued and fascinated by the concepts of soul love and soul mates and you are in tune with your destiny. You are in touch with your feelings and your emotions. You are very allowing of all that happens in life and the people you meet. You are not resistant to what happens. You like light, you like sparkles and you probably like fairies!

This music seems to show you a vision of how life can really be, and it is a beautiful vision. A vision full of harmony, openness, appreciation and allowing. These are higher vibrational qualities. You are a happy soul, but you could benefit from more people to connect to on this vibrational level.

You see the beauty in life.

A beautiful song and a beautiful you!

Client Feedback

"Hi Awen,

Thank you so much for taking the time for analyzing my song. I told a friend to write you as well.

The best of all!"

Lucy

CHAPTER FIFTY-THREE

"To Be with You" performed by Mr Big

If this is your favorite song, then you are probably special in these ways:

- Peaceful
- Enjoy connecting with people and enjoy camaraderie
- Understand that you are a child of the world
- Have a sunny disposition
- Optimistic
- Appreciative
- Have a youthful attitude
- Possess clarity
- Value yourself
- A giver and give words of appreciation and encouragement
- A good friend
- Supportive
- Open to love and romance
- A good cheerleader for humanity
- Special

Client: Madison

It has been a pleasure to intuit this Song Read for you.

I interpret your deeper connection to the song in this way:

You want to exist with humanity in peace, connected in mutual appreciation. You enjoy connecting with people, your friends and family. You understand that you are a child of the world, and not somehow apart from it. You see no reason to live in the way that "every man is an island." That would be senseless to you.

You have a sunny disposition. You are pleasant and pleasing and optimistic. You appreciate many of the simple things in life. I get the feeling that you are a young person, or if not, you have a youthful quality to you. You have a youthful attitude! You are clear and have clarity. The Spring season comes to mind. You are like Spring—the new air, the new colors, the new fragrances. You have a nice open crown chakra showing your easy connection with all that is.

You have perhaps been a little hurt, as we have all been. But you seem to be very much over this. You have had some blues, but you are over this too. You value yourself. Whatever hardships you have had, you have learned to value yourself. Old remnants of hurt sometimes block your upper arms. This is shown by a little bit of heavy energy in the upper arms. The upper arms are connected by meridians to the heart chakra, which is where the old hurt comes from. So if you sometimes become aware of uncomfortable heavy energy in the upper arms just breathe in and release it out from the upper arm muscles.

You are a great giver. You give to others very easily and generously. You also give words of appreciation and encouragement and support. You are well liked for this. Whatever difficulties the lyrics allude to, you have overcome them, and this is an achievement. You are a good friend and you support your friends.

You like the clapping in the music. The joining in of the group and how everybody has a sound to bring to the whole. You enjoy the sense of camaraderie of clapping together.

You like love. You are open to love. You like romance. You like goodness and you really appreciate it if somebody compliments you or appreciates you.

You are a good cheerleader for humanity. You love humanity and you enjoy being a part of the human race.

The message in the music for you is this: You are special. Appreciate the specialness of you.

Bless you.

CHAPTER FIFTY-FOUR

"Vision of Division" performed by The Strokes

If this is your favorite song, then you are probably special in these ways:

- Sensitive
- Sensitive to the mass thought-forms of society
- Passionate
- Desire to be happy and free
- Willing to be open
- Willing to be responsible
- Possess a hidden gift

Client: Philip

Thank you for the opportunity to intuit this Song Read for you. I had not heard this music before.

I interpret your deeper connection to the song in this way:

There is some confusion and you are a bit surprised! (I think of a rabbit in headlights.) Perhaps at times you have ended up in the wrong situation with the wrong people, and you are frustrated by this. But there is a silver lining. By understanding that you've been in the wrong situation with the wrong people, you can now learn from this and seek out better people, better situations.

You are sensitive, and you pick up a lot of the mass thought-forms of society. This naturally creates a bit of confusion for you. Sometimes you are not in your own thoughts but are experiencing the thoughts of others. And so, not surprisingly, you appear to be quite a restless soul. I receive the feeling that this song will move away from you within a certain time frame. I don't think that this is a song which you are going to carry through life. I think this is a song you like, but I don't think it is your favorite song. I think this song will drop off from you as you age.

There seems to be quite a bit of passion, some impatience and some irritation at not being understood. But for you to be understood, you must realize the need to offer understanding to other people. Then it becomes a mutual-reciprocal empowering vibe.

You want to be happy and free. With the guitar sounds, I sense a hidden gift in you waiting to be discovered.

A little quiet will give you a welcome sense of peace and respite from the noise of others.

The title of this song says much. There seems to be a challenge to accept the responsibility and to put into action your own self-determination, rather than lashing out at others who have caused pain. This challenge is a very common theme for many of us. It is helpful for us to halt our blaming and accept responsibility for the perspectives we choose to employ. When we take responsibility for ourselves, there is often a gradual and harmonious change to a new, more empowering perspective. I have great hope for you, because you are showing your willingness to be open and responsible.

Client Feedback

"Thanks for interpreting my favorite song at the moment. I think you made some very interesting points. By the way I play in a rock band. I'd love to hear which songs give you a positive vibe."—Philip

CHAPTER FIFTY-FIVE

"What You Want" performed by Evanescence

If this is your favorite song, then you are probably special in these ways:

- Intellectual
- Clever
- Rational and logical
- Analytical
- Easily solve complex problems
- Have a reservoir of energy at your disposal
- Have a storehouse of knowledge
- Connected to physical world
- Desire to make a statement
- Enjoy words
- Able to get things done
- Potential for emotional and intuitive capabilities

Client: Mikaela

It has been a pleasure to intuit this Song Read for you. I had not heard this music before.

I interpret your deeper connection to the song in this way:

You have a strong intellectual, rational, analytical, logical side. You enjoy complex problems and are able to solve them. You express a lot of energy and have a reservoir of energy at your disposal. You also have a storehouse of knowledge.

You seem to spend a lot of time in your thoughts. There is some defiance and anger in you, a crossness, but it appears to be more of a front, an image you present to the world. You do not like to be controlled.

Your crown chakra is quite activated, so this music connects you with Source. I sense that you connect to the lyrics. The music is very much of this Earth. It is physical and you are possibly very physical too. You seem to have a desire to make a statement. I sense that you are intellectual and enjoy words. You express your creativity through your intellect and you may also be talented at math. You operate more in your thinking body than your feeling body. You are no doubt a clever person. You are a thinker and you appreciate the lyrics.

The lyrics are helpful for you and they can guide you. The lyrics also have a possible spiritual element to them. What seems to happen in your energy field is that your intellect and your love of meaning in words and your love of understanding push out and overtakes your emotional and intuitive capabilities. So your creativity has difficulty expressing in these areas. Your creativity expresses rather through your intellect. You are exceedingly strong in your intellect. Many people would connect to these lyrics through emotions or their intuition. You may be relying too heavily on the left brain because it works so successfully for you. You appear to be exceedingly clever, analytical and able to get things done. But you have other faculties of emotions and intuition which you may like to develop as well. And these faculties are available to you. Your enjoyment of these lyrics suggests that you are open to discovering these other sides of your personality.

The Collins Australian Dictionary defines evanescence as "quickly fading away, ephemeral or transitory." This perhaps suggests qualities of intuition and clairvoyance

CHAPTER FIFTY-SIX

"With or Without You" performed by U2

If this is your favorite song, then you are probably special in these ways:

- Aware of life all around
- Receptive
- Spiritual
- Joyful and loving
- Hopeful
- Drawn to a sense of awe
- Appreciate beauty
- Determined
- Naturally listen to your gut feelings
- Open hearted and openly express emotions
- Have trust and faith
- Have an understanding of ultimate love
- Understand that surrender brings growth
- Open to vulnerability
- Talented at relationships
- Optimistic, patient and generous

Client: Dean

It has been a pleasure to intuit this Song Read for you.

lI interpret your deeper connection to the song in this way:

These are the impressions I receive: The harmonies, the ache, the impression of this ache, and the awareness of life all around you, the energy all around you. Overtones of religion. Jesus. Somebody kneeling and praying. You possess a wonderfully clear energy field, very open, very receptive. You are probably a spiritual person. You are a joyful, hopeful, beautifully open person who is open to awe and open to beauty.

The fullness of the music is very beautiful. There is a determination, a knowing what is right, and of listening to your gut feelings and being happy to do this.

I actually see two people, arms stretched out, twirling around, up in the sky. There could be a deeper spiritual overtone. Talking to spirit, talking to your higher self. There is a lot of joy. The guitar sounds like spiritual bells ringing your welcome home. You have an incredibly open energy field, big, light, chakras full of energy, a lot of goodness, a lot of heart, a lot of love, strongly connected to The Divine, and you can easily pull down energy from the heavens. There is great joy here for you.

The guitar sounds are like angels talking to you, they sound like the angels dancing with you. I have the impression that you are not completely aware of what I am discussing here, that possibly you see only glimpses of this.

Tears of pain, also tears of joy. You openly express your emotions. I sense some stinging pain behind your eyes. Maybe you have suffered a loss. Faith, you have faith. You trust people. For you there is a deeper significance to the title of this song. There is a deep inner meaning to this line which you have locked up. You haven't quite unlocked the meaning of this line for yourself yet. You seem to have an understanding of ultimate love. You like the song lyrics. You may have experienced romantic heartbreak, but that is not what the song means for you. It is not the romantic heartbreak. This music possibly talks about your relationship with Spirit. All of your upper chakras are rejoicing. There is a rejoicing quality to that fantastic guitar sound. Your crown chakra is open and wants to clap! You are very connected.to Source. I sense a deeper vision, a deeper understanding, within you, but this is still quite locked away at the moment. You understand the necessity of surrendering to The Divine; you understand that surrender actually brings growth.

You are an emotional person and can easily express your emotions. You connect at times with people who don't appreciate your vulnerability. But by being vulnerable, we open ourselves up to love. Perhaps some of the people you connect with are more guarded, less confident to engage on such an intimate level. You are talented at relationships but sometimes want too much from the other person (as in, heart and soul). It is possible that you trust too easily. Sometimes you don't pay enough attention to the details. Perhaps you do not read some of the spiritual signs in front of you. These signs are showing you where a situation is going to end up.

Maybe you sometimes criticize others. Sometimes you don't feel connected to other people down here on the physical plane. And it is likely that this criticism of others is really a consequence of some of your own pain. However the criticism is more in your past and you are moving away from it.

The music helps you to soar high; it creates optimism and hope for you. These qualities are within you too, along with patience and generosity. This music speaks to so many of us on a collective level. The music connects us with Source.

I receive the sense of you dancing, swaying, with your palms up. The music very much connects you to Source. I pick up Spirit coming down from the heavens, traveling right through your body and entering the Earth.

This music overwhelms you with love and connection. You remember the love of "all that is."

ABOUT THE AUTHOR

AWEN FINN

Awen Finn was born in the United Kingdom and began her career in fashion before moving to Australia in 1989. In Sydney, Awen went on to develop a successful business in the art world, co-founding art galleries and a successful art publishing company.

Awen began her journey in spirituality after attending a meditation class with a friend. She went on to train and qualify as an energy healer and spiritual teacher before she began to understand the incredible connection hidden within music and the spiritual energy of the world. She now interprets how to apply this life-changing knowledge in people's favorite songs while completely transforming their understanding of music and its energy.

To get the latest Read My Song, Read My Heart, Read My Soul updates and resources, visit:

ReadMySongReadMySoul.com

You can also connect with Awen here:

Blog: ReadMySongReadMySoul.com
Twitter: @ReadMySong

ACKNOWLEDGMENTS

My deepest thanks to my first spiritual teachers, my parents Frances and Thomas, and for all you've given me.

My very special thanks to my partner, my son and my daughter for bringing love and laughter to my life and for showing me some of the spiritual range of incarnation into this physical world. Thank you Dave for your support and encouragement and for being there at the start of this project, and thank you so much Berwyn for your helpful suggestions.

A big thank you to my spiritual teachers who have guided me. Thank you to Shakti Durga for your energy, enlightenment, healing and inclusiveness of love. To John and James, thank you for your teaching and for your friendship. Thank you James for always having the exact book recommendation ready for when I needed it the most! My very special thanks to Paramahansa Yogananda and Sri Yukteswar. An enormous thank you for your teaching, guidance and for accompanying me on this journey.

Thank you to The Divine for working through me.

I have a special gratitude in my heart for all of the wonderful song writers, composers and musicians whose songs are referred to in these pages. I am in awe of your talents—truly in awe. Thank you.

And most of all, I would like to thank all of the many people who contributed their favorite songs to the pages of this book. Without the help of these individuals, who so generously shared their favorite songs, this book could never have been written. Their support for my efforts means more to me than I can express

.

THANK YOU!

Thank you for buying and reading this book and trusting me to offer something of value. I'd be thrilled to hear from you with your favorite songs. You can go to my blog, readmysongreadmysoul.com and click on the 'Contact" button! I also hope you'll consider subscribing to my blog at readmysongreadmysoul.com It would be a huge honor if you decide to subscribe! That would prove this book had a positive impact on you!

Wishing you love and joy, always!

Awen